The Future of the Multinational Enterprise

Second Edition

Peter J. Buckley
Professor of Managerial Economics
University of Bradford Management Centre

and

Mark Casson
Professor of Economics
University of Reading

MACMILLAN

First edition 1976
Reprinted 1978
Second edition 1991

Published by
THE MACMILLAN PRESS LTD
Houndmills, Basingstoke, Hampshire RG21 2XS
and London
Companies and representatives
throughout the world

Printed in Hong Kong

British Library Cataloguing in Publication Data
Buckley, Peter J. (Peter Jenning) *1949–*
The future of the multinational enterprise.
1. Multinational companies
I. Title
338.88
ISBN 0–333–53888–9 (hardcover)
ISBN 0–333–49249–8 (paperback)

For Janet

Contents

Contents

Introduction to the Second Edition

The Future of the Multinational Enterprise on its publication in 1976 contained the provocative statement that 'It is little exaggeration to say that at present there is no established theory of the multinational enterprise.' This was bound to raise a few hackles and duly did so. A prompt review in *The Journal of Management Studies* by V. N. Balasubramanyam began: 'Buckley and Casson have no patience with orthodoxy' (p. 307), and cast some doubt about the book's claim to originality. The claims to originality and generality despite the books' being 'both rigorously and vigorously argued' were judged not to have been fully met by Stephen Kobrin (1977, p. 137). Rugman, later to become a champion of internalisation as an approach to the analysis of multinational firms, felt that the claim to have developed a general theory of the multinational enterprise 'is not entirely unjustified and their book may well come to be accepted as the definitive synthesis on the motives for foreign direct investment' (1977, p. 410).

The first public airings of the concepts underlying the book were at a staff seminar of the Department of Economics at Reading and the Annual Meeting of the UK Region of the Academy of International Business (AIB), also at Reading, in May 1975. At the AIB meeting the paper was described as 'the lightning rod of the conference' by Bob Hawkins. The concepts were then presented at the Academy of International Business's Conference at INSEAD, Fontainebleau, France in July 1975, a paper which was published as 'A Theory of International Operations' (1978). In general, initial response was enthusiastic, but cautious.

Since then, the book has been widely cited as a basic source of the internalisation approach to the theory of the multinational enterprise. The Social Science citation index lists over 100 citations (1988).

However, much of the impact of the book has been mediated through other authors, notably John Dunning and Alan Rugman. Dunning's 'eclectic theory' drew on the concepts of location and internalisation but added a third key variable, ownership advantages. These large-scale organising principles were used by Dunning as a framework for the analysis not only of the operations of multinational firms, but also of resource flows outside the firm, the role of foreign investment in development and policy-related issues (Dunning 1981). The separate and independent existence of ownership advantages in a dynamic context has been a matter of debate ever since (Casson 1987, Chapter 2).

Conversely, Alan Rugman collapsed the explanatory dyad of internationalisation and location factors into a single all-embracing concept of internalisation. Locational factors were subsumed by the inclusion of 'spatial cost saving' as a firm specific advantage which is of benefit only when internalised (1981, p. 48).

Some subsequent work has sought to differentiate the approach of *The Future* . . . from that of Rugman and Dunning and to emphasise its superiority. These issues have been termed 'family quarrels' by Alan Rugman. See Buckley (1983b; 1988a), Casson (1987, Chapter 2), Dunning (1988) for example.

The final point leads to the view of an 'extended family' arising from what, for convenient shorthand, has been described as the Reading School. Not all the debate has been inward looking. Attempts have been made to contrast the various Reading approaches with:

(i)   the work of Hymer and the market imperfections approach (Dunning and Rugman 1985); and

(ii) Aliber's approach, based on foreign currency areas (Aliber 1970; 1971), and Kojima's work which contrasts 'US type' foreign direct investment with the 'Japanese type' (Kojima 1978; 1982), Buckley (1983a; 1985).

There is a sense in which the work contained in *The Future* . . . is not a complete theory but rather the core of a general approach to multinational firms and their near relations

– a theme taken up by Buckley (1988). It is not only the system of concepts and the particular insights which are crucial, but an appropriate method of analysis. This method of analysis was early on felt to apply not only to the multinational firm itself and to foreign direct investment but also to the alternatives to the multinational firm (the title of Casson's next (1979) book) – licensing, management contracts, technology agreements, subcontracting etc. The robust nature of the concepts was subsequently demonstrated by the ability to analyse these alternative contractual arrangements (Casson 1979, Buckley and Casson 1985, Chapter 3). The move away from the analysis of the institution – the multinational firm – to modes of (international) contracting was facilitated by the transactions-based core of the theory. The integration with the theory of international trade which is now an important and exciting research frontier (Krugman 1979 and 1981, Helpman 1984, Ethier 1986, among others) is a culmination of this direction of research.

Naturally, *The Future of the Multinational Enterprise* was not the only use of the original concept of Ronald Coase (1937) in the analysis of the multinational firm. The approach was also independently utilised by McManus (1972), Baumann (1975), Wilson Brown (1976), Swedenborg (1979) and Hennart (1982).

Perhaps a strength of *The Future*. . .'s particular approach, *pace* some reviewers, was that it did not deviate greatly from orthodoxy. Its approach could be described as largely conventional. The marginal calculus is retained and profit maximisation remains the sole objective of the firm. The nature of the imperfections in the external market is made explicit, and the firm's response is to grope towards internal markets to replace the more costly external ones. Because imperfections in external markets are observable and systematic in their incidence, the direction of the growth of the firm is predictable. Consequently, the use of certain 'stylised facts' enables the testing of broad tendencies in the pattern of growth, industrial distribution, nationality of ownership and multinationality of multinational firms. From an explanation of these stylised facts it is possible to go on to test the additional predictions of the theory.

In fact, *The Future*. . . did more than that. With the help of Bob Pearce, it was possible to use the data assembled by Bob and John Dunning to test – admittedly rather indirectly – some of the main propositions of a key special theory: the case of R&D–intensive multinationals. One of the continuing criticisms of the whole approach has been the difficulties of testing. It is undeniable that a search for proxies has had to be undertaken and that the design of crucial experiments is not easy. However, results to date show that the theory has survived a number of significant attempts to refute it.

The emphasis on key exogenous factors driving the growth of the firm moved the study of international business away from straight line projections of the growth and dominance of large firms towards a more balanced view of growth under constraints arising from predictable external influences. Disintegration, too, is raised as a possibility, e.g. through a shift towards licensing.

The relationship between the 'internalisation' approach and the markets and hierarchies approach of Oliver Williamson (1975; 1985) has been the subject of attention. Many similarities are evident, but it is worth emphasising the differences (see also Buckley 1988b). Hierarchy is presented as an alternative to the market by Williamson as a means of monitoring and motivating individuals. It is felt to be a superior mode of organisation in situations where market-based incentives cannot fully specify all the tasks. Where uncertainty and complexity dominate the environment, hierarchy thus becomes the best means of reducing the 'governance costs' of managing a team of individuals.

The internalisation approach to multinationals emphasised at an early stage that authority relations are not the only means of resolving the problems of maintaining individuals within the organisation and reducing governance costs. Managers of foreign subsidiaries usually have better knowledge of local conditions than central management and thus it may be difficult to use traditional forms of authority to remove their discretion in decision making. Better results may be achieved by altering the incentives to individuals through the imposition of a decentralised system of shadow pricing. This will constrain the managers of individual units to act as profit centres in responding to the internal prices set by top managers in line with the firm's overall objectives.

Despite such differences of emphasis, the approaches are

complementary in two important ways: first, they share the view that organisations economise on transaction costs; second, they require the use of supporting assumptions to give empirical content. Much of the empirical content derives from assumptions about the relative incidence of transactions costs in internal and external markets. Problems in the definition and measurement of transaction costs have not yet been fully resolved; in particular the magnitude of these costs in relation to production, transport, marketing and distribution – as well as their spatial configuration – remains to be specified in detail.

The Future of the Multinational Enterprise provided a succinct statement of theory which enabled the synthesis of several important previous works – Vernon on the Product Cycle, Kindleberger and Caves on market imperfections, Aliber on currency area effects, behavioural work on the process of direct investment and portfolio approaches to diversification. It also had the virtue of providing a research agenda. It gave a stimulus to the synthesising work which John Dunning was undertaking and allowed a successful reintegration of previous empirical work, notably Dunning's pioneering work (1958) into the mainstream of theory.

The research agenda has by no means worked itself out. The integration of institutionalist and neo-classical elements is by no means complete and the continuing rediscovery of the importance of institutionalist concepts (including the renewed interest in Richardson's 1972 article) attests to this (Buckley 1989). The modelling of dynamics is by no means complete and the issue of how best to deal with dynamic issues lies at the root of much of the current intra-Reading and extra-Reading controversies. The reintegration of the theory of the multinational enterprise with the theory of finance, the theory of international trade and locational economics continues apace but is not yet complete.

Peter J. Buckley
Mark Casson
1990

REFERENCES

Aliber, Robert Z. (1970) 'A Theory of Direct Foreign Investment', in C. P. Kindleberger (ed.) *The International Firm* (Cambridge, Mass: MIT Press), pp. 17–34.

Aliber, Robert Z. (1971) 'The Multinational Enterprise in a Multiple Currency World', in John H. Dunning (ed.) *The Multinational Enterprise* (London: George Allen & Unwin), pp. 49–56.

Balasubramanyam, V. N. (1976) 'The Multinationals', *Journal of Management Studies* 13, 305–11.

Baumann, H. G. (1975) 'Merger Theory, Property Rights and the Pattern of US Direct Investment in Canada', *Weltwirtschaftliches Archiv*, 111, 676–98.

Brown, Wilson R. (1976) 'Islands of Conscious Power: MNCs in the Theory of the Firm', *MSU Business Topics*, 24, 37–45.

Buckley, Peter J. (1983a) 'New Theories of International Business: Some Unresolved Issues', in Mark Casson (ed.) *The Growth of International Business* (London: George Allen & Unwin), pp. 34–50.

Buckley, Peter J. (1983b) 'Macroeconomic versus the International Business Approach to Direct Foreign Investment: A Comment on Professor Kojima's Approach', *Hitotsubashi Journal of Economics*, 21, 395–400.

Buckley, Peter J. (1985) 'The Economic Analysis of the Multinational Enterprise: Reading versus Japan?', *Hitotsubashi Journal of Economics*, 26, 117–24.

Buckley, Peter J. (1988a) 'The Limits of Explanation: Testing the Internalisation Theory of the Multinational Enterprise', *Journal of International Business Studies*, XIX, 181–93.

Buckley, Peter J. (1988b) 'Organisational Forms and Multinational Companies', in Steve Thompson and Mike Wright (eds) *Internal Organisation, Efficiency and Profit* (Oxford: Philip Allan).

Buckley, Peter J. (1989) 'The Institutionalist Perspective on Recent Theories of Foreign Direct Investment: A Comment on McClintock', *Journal of Institutional Economics* (forthcoming).

Buckley, Peter J. and Mark Casson (1978) 'A Theory of International Operations', in Michael Ghertman and James Leontiadis *European Research in International Business* (Amsterdam: North-Holland), pp. 1–8.

Buckley, Peter J. and Mark Casson (1985) *The Economic Analysis of the Multinational Enterprise: Selected Papers* (London: Macmillan).

Casson, Mark (1979) *Alternatives to the Multinational Enterprise* (London: Macmillan).

Casson, Mark (1987) *The Firm and the Market* (London: George Allen & Unwin).

Coase, Ronald H. (1937) 'The Nature of the Firm', *Economica* (New Series) 4, 386–405.

Dunning, John H. (1981) *International Production and the Multinational Enterprise* (London: George Allen & Unwin).

Dunning, John H. (1988) 'The Eclectic Paradigm of International Production: A Restatement and Some Possible Extensions', *Journal of International Business Studies*, XIX, 1–32.

Dunning, John H. and Alan M. Rugman (1985) 'The Influence of Hymer's Dissertation on the Theory of Foreign Direct Investment', *American Economic Review*, 75, 228–32.

Ethier, Wilfred J. (1986) 'The Multinational Firm', *Quarterly Journal of Economics*, CI, 805–33.

Helpman, Elhanan (1984) 'A Simple Theory of International Trade with Multinational Corporations', *Journal of Political Economy*, 92, 451–71.

Hennart, Jean-François (1982) A Theory of Multinational Enterprise (Ann Arbor: University of Michigan Press).

Kobrin, Stephen J. (1977) 'The Future of the Multinational Enterprise: Review', *Journal of Marketing*, 41, 137–8.

Kojima, K. (1978) *Direct Foreign Investment: A Japanese Model of Multinational Business Operations* (London: Croom Helm).

Kojima, K. (1982) 'Macroeconomic versus International Business Approach to Direct Foreign Investment', *Hitotsubashi Journal of Economics*, 23, 1–19.

Krugman, Paul (1979) 'Increasing Returns, Monopolistic Competition and International Trade', *Journal of International Economics*, 9, 469–80.

Krugman, Paul (1983) 'The New Theories of International Trade and the Multinational Enterprise', in Charles P. Kindleberger and David Audretch (eds) *The Multinational Corporation in the 1980s* (Cambridge, Mass: MIT Press), pp. 57–73.

McManus, John C. (1972) 'The Theory of the International Firm', in Gilles Paquet (ed.) *The Multinational Firm and the Nation State* (Toronto: Collier-Macmillan), pp. 66–93.

Richardson, D. B. (1972) 'The Organisation of Industry', *Economic Journal*, 82, 883–96.

Rugman, Alan M. (1977) 'Do Multinationals have a Future?' *Futures* 9, 243–6.

Rugman, Alan M. (1981) *Inside the Multinationals* (London: Croom Helm).

Swedenborg, Briggitta (1979) Multinational Operations of Swedish Firms (Stockholm: Almquist & Wiksell).

Williamson, Oliver E. (1975) *Markets and Hierarchies: Analysis and Anti Trust Implications* (New York: Free Press).

Williamson, Oliver E. (1985) *The Economic Institutions of Capitalism: Firms, Markets and Relational Contracting* (New York: Free Press).

Preface

A recent writer on business economics (Frederick Scherer) addresses his book to 'bright, well-motivated laymen ... most of the time I have in mind Supreme Court clerks as the reader'. It is our hope that the Supreme Court clerks will enjoy reading the present work as well. Because this book has a simple but important point to make with respect to the origins and future growth of multinational enterprises, the main onus on the reader is to follow through the logic of the argument without necessarily mastering the technical detail. We have produced ample supporting evidence of a statistical nature, which we believe will interest managers, civil servants, politicians and academics; however, the evidence has been documented in such a way that it does not detract from the gist of the argument as perceived by the non-technical reader.

Chapter 1 presents the background to the study, summarising and interpreting the most recent evidence on the participation of multinational enterprises in the world economy. The discussion highlights several key characteristics of multinational enterprises which require explanation.

Chapter 2 shows how these characteristics can be explained by the concept of *internalisation*. The concept was introduced forty years ago by Ronald Coase, but it is only recently that its full importance has been recognised; the concept provides a link between the economic theory of markets and managerial theories of organisation and control. It is argued that the growth of the multinational enterprise is governed basically by the costs and benefits of internalising markets. We suggest that in the first phase of the growth of the multinational enterprise (up to the end of the Second World War) the dominant pressure for internalisation was the need of large firms and advanced economies to regulate future supplies of raw materials. After the Second World War the dominant force was the need to diffuse technical and marketing know-how in a way which best maintained the innovating firm's proprietary rights.

Chapter 3 reviews alternative theories of the multinational enterprise, and shows how many of them can be synthesised within the theoretical framework developed in Chapter 2.

Chapter 4 tests the main predictions of the theory against the measured behaviour of a sample of over four hundred of the world's largest manufacturing firms. It is shown that the theory can explain a great deal about the multinationality, growth, profitability and research-intensity of large firms.

Chapter 5 shows how the theory can be used to predict the future pattern of multinationalism. It is argued that at the present state of development of the multinational enterprise the dominant force for internalisation is undergoing change. The advantages of internalising specialised technical know-how are diminishing relative to the advantages of internalising general marketing expertise. As the balance of advantages shifts, certain types of multinational enterprise are going into decline while others are steadily increasing in importance. It is argued that conventional policy prescriptions may have to be revised in the light of this changing structure of multinationalism.

This book was begun on a summer holiday which the authors enjoyed in the company of Richard Cohen, to whom they are eternally grateful for his good humour, and exceptional qualities of endurance. The idea were written up on our return to Bradford and Reading respectively. We are grateful to Professor John Dunning, Tom Parry, Bob Pearce and David Robertson for constructive criticisms of earlier drafts. Professor Dunning and Bob Pearce also kindly made available to us their data on the world's largest firms; Michele Foot programmed our calculations with quite remarkable efficiency. We should also like to thank Pru Christmas, Margaret Lewis, Joan Kew and Sylvia Lee for their typing of the manuscript.

Parts of the book have been given at seminars in Bradford and Reading, and to conferences in Reading and Fontainebleau, and we are grateful to the discussants for their comments and

criticisms. We have also benefited from discussions with Nils
Lundgren and Bernard Wolf, who have been working along
similar lines to ourselves.

September 1975 P.J.B.
M.C.

The authors and publishers wish to thank Harvard University
Press for permission to use extracts from tables in *The World's
Multinational Enterprises* by James W. Vaupel and Joan P.
Curhan.

1 The Multinational Enterprise in the World Economy

1.1 Introduction

One of the most remarkable economic phenomena of the post-war period has been the rise of the multinational enterprise (MNE). An MNE may be defined as an enterprise which owns and controls activities in different countries. No economic organisation in post-industrial society has evolved so quickly and to such a high degree of sophistication as the MNE. The closest parallels are to the trusts and cartels which rose to prominence about the turn of the century. But these were only national in scale, their international operations being governed by a loose federation of business leaders rather than by direct control from a corporate world headquarters. The growth of the cartels was responsible for an increase in government participation in economic life through the enactment of anti-trust laws; it also inspired the development of the economic theory of imperfect competition, which revolutionised economic thinking on the basic issue of resource allocation. Something of a similar revolution is required today. The growth of the MNE has caught both governments and economists unawares. Governments organised on a national scale find it difficult to exert controls or sanctions against international firms, since competition between host nations for the benefits of foreign direct investment ensures that a restrictive policy toward MNEs will only succeed in driving out foreign investors to a more favourable climate. The most effective method of control is for governments to agree upon a new industrial policy which can be policed on a supranational basis. However, a prerequisite

1

of an effective policy is an understanding of the behaviour of MNEs. It is unfortunate that in this respect orthodox economic theory is not very helpful. The theories of imperfect competition which explained the behaviour of the trusts must be reformulated and extended before they can be applied to the MNE. A step in this direction has been made by writers such as Hymer and Kindleberger, though as we shall show, in its present state their theory has relatively little predictive power. It is the object of this book to provide a theory of the MNE which is sufficiently powerful to afford long-term projections of the future growth and structure of MNEs. It is hoped that the theory can be used as the basis for a rational economic policy toward the MNE, which will preserve the benefits conferred by these giant firms, while restoring effective social and political control over their operations.

Theories cannot be developed in a vacuum, so in this introductory chapter we present an historical perspective of the growth of MNEs, together with recent evidence on their structure. The statistics summarised in this chapter highlight several key features of the MNE which any satisfactory theory must explain.

1.2   The growth of MNEs

Table 1.1 and Figs. 1.1 to 1.4 exhibit the growth of overseas operations of MNEs since 1914. The figures show the average number of subsidiaries formed per annum plotted on a logarithmic scale against time. A constant proportional rate of increase over time appears on the graph as a straight line sloping upward from left to right. The fact that most of the graphs increase in slope very markedly from 1946–52 onwards enables us to date the 'take-off' of the MNEs to just after the end of the Second World War. Four separate groups of data have been graphed, relating respectively to MNEs based in the US, UK, continental Europe and Japan. The four groups of data are not strictly comparable: data for the US relate to the 187 largest industrial firms manufacturing in six or more foreign countries in 1963; the smallest of these firms had sales of about $100 million in 1968, and as a group they account for about 70 per cent of US foreign direct investment in manufacturing. Data for the

TABLE 1.1 Average number of new subsidiaries formed per annum by geographical area, for four groups of parent companies based respectively in the US, UK, continental Europe and Japan, 1914–70.

	1914–19	1920–9	1930–8	1939–45	1946–52	1953–5	1956–8	1959–61	1962–4	1965–7	1968–70
US-based parents											
Canada	5.3	8.4	7.7	5.7	12.1	20.8	20.5	29.7	32.0	32.6	
South America	2.0	3.9	7.4	11.8	17.4	30.1	55.2	78.4	67.1	74.4	
Europe	1.7	9.2	8.6	2.1	10.9	20.6	31.3	102.1	111.6	99.6	na
UK	0.8	4.8	6.0	1.7	6.1	7.0	12.7	28.2	27.5	26.1	
Africa	0.2	0.5	1.4	0.7	2.2	3.7	6.7	9.0	23.3	11.0	
Asia and Pacific	1.8	3.0	3.7	2.6	6.9	12.7	19.8	53.2	54.7	50.7	
Total	11.8	29.9	35.0	24.6	55.1	94.3	146.3	300.3	319.7	296.3	
UK-based parents											
US and Canada	0.5	1.8	1.0	0.1	2.6	3.4	12.9	14.0	10.9	22.3	37.9
South America	0.7	1.4	0.7	0.4	0.9	2.6	2.4	7.7	4.1	6.7	10.7
Europe	1.0	4.6	4.6	0.7	3.8	2.3	3.4	32.3	29.8	44.0	73.4
Africa	0.5	1.6	1.0	1.0	11.8	4.4	4.4	23.6	27.1	33.7	56.9
Asia and Pacific	1.8	2.4	3.6	2.3	10.1	5.7	8.3	32.8	33.6	46.7	60.5
Total	4.5	11.8	11.0	4.8	28.8	18.3	31.3	111.0	106.3	153.0	243.0
Continental European parents											
US and Canada	1.5	2.7	0.9	0.4	1.6	5.6	6.3	16.7	10.8	20.7	48.1
South America	0.3	1.5	1.8	0.6	4.3	7.7	–9.4	10.0	10.3	25.2	43.2
Europe	5.9	16.5	7.1	4.1	7.9	16.1	15.9	24.4	34.1	81.0	179.2
UK	0.8	1.8	1.6	0.7	2.2	3.7	6.3	7.3	26.6	26.6	22.3
Africa	0.0	0.4	0.0	0.1	1.6	2.7	3.7	10.0	3.9	12.8	25.4
Asia and Pacific	0.0	1.7	0.8	0.3	1.0	3.4	4.6	10.0	9.9	12.2	26.1
Total	8.5	24.9	12.4	6.3	18.4	39.0	43.7	77.3	76.3	177.3	343.3
Japanese parents											
US and Canada	0.0	0.0	0.0	0.3	0.0	0.0	0.0	0.3	1.0	3.0	2.7
South America	0.0	0.0	0.1	0.0	0.0	0.7	3.3	1.7	4.6	9.3	7.5
Europe	0.0	0.0	0.0	0.1	0.0	0.0	0.0	0.7	1.7	0.3	3.0
UK	0.0	0.0	0.0	0.0	0.0	0.0	0.0	0.3	0.0	0.0	0.0
Africa	0.0	0.0	0.0	0.0	0.0	0.0	0.7	3.3	0.0	3.1	3.1
Asia and Pacific	0.0	0.1	0.2	5.3	0.3	1.0	1.0	11.1	19.1	22.2	53.2
Total	0.0	0.1	0.3	5.7	0.3	1.7	4.7	14.7	30.0	37.7	70.0

Source: J. W. Vaupel and J. P. Curhan, *The World's Multinational Enterprises* (Geneva, 1974), Tables 1.17.2–5.
Notes: See text, and Vaupel and Curhan, pp. 1–18. Europe includes Scandinavia and Israel.

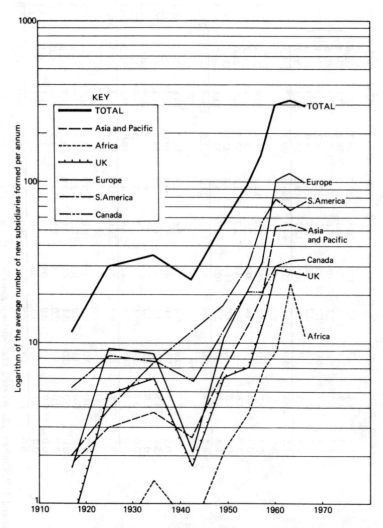

F<small>IG</small>. 1.1 Average number of new subsidiaries formed per annum by geographical
area, for a sample of 187 US-based parent MNEs, 1914–70.
Source for Figs. 1.1–4: J. W. Vaupel and J. P. Curhan, *The World's Multinational
Enterprises* (Geneva, 1974).

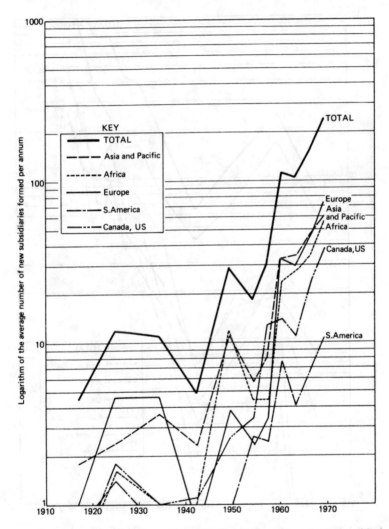

FIG. 1.2 Average number of new subsidiaries formed per annum by geographical area, for a sample of UK-based MNEs among the 200 largest non-US industrial firms, 1914–70.

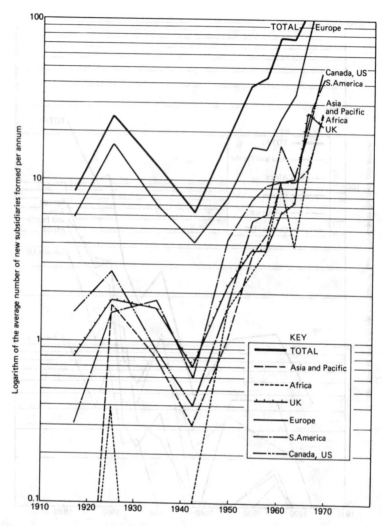

FIG. 1.3 Average number of new subsidiaries formed per annum by geographical area, for a sample of continental European-based MNEs among the 200 largest non-US industrial firms, 1914–70.

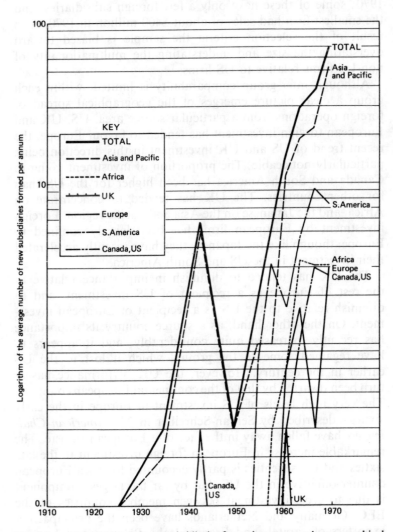

FIG. 1.4 Average number of new subsidiaries formed per annum by geographical area, for sample of Japanese-based MNEs among the 200 largest non-US industrial firms, 1914–70.

non-US firms concern basically the 200 largest industrial firms in 1970; some of these have only a few foreign subsidiaries, and the smallest firm had sales of about $400 million in 1970. As a result of the selection criteria the sample is biased toward overstating the size and understating the multinationality of non-US firms relative to US firms.

Although inter-group comparability is limited, within each group a clear picture emerges of the geographical spread of foreign operations from a particular source area. US, UK and European foreign investment has tended to favour Europe, the recent trend of US and UK investment in this direction being particularly noticeable. The proportion of investment going to Canada and South America has been higher for the US than for other countries. The UK has tended to concentrate on Africa, and the Japanese on the Asia and Pacific region. Foreign investment by European firms has been largely confined to Europe, though like the Japanese they have recently accelerated their investment in the US and South America.

The UK has tended to diminish in importance relative to the rest of Europe as a recipient of US investment, and to diminish relative to the US as a recipient of European invest- ment. On the other hand, as a source country its importance has recently increased quite considerably, and it appears to have regained some of the ground which it lost to the US earlier in the century. However, the UK performance has in turn been dwarfed by that of the continental European countries. The very high levels of US investment in Europe in the early sixties -- described by Servan-Schreiber in *The American Chal- lenge* – have fallen away in the face of a European riposte. The remarkable increase in European foreign investment in the late sixties and the seventies is partly accounted for by a European counter-offensive in the US, but by far the largest component is due to cross-investment between member countries of the EEC. Germany and Netherlands have been the principal net exporters of capital, and France, Italy, Belgium and Luxem- bourg the net importers.[1]

[1] See M. Holthus and G. Koopman, *The Extent and Importance of the Opera- tions of the Multinational Firms in the EEC*, mimeo (Hamburg: Institute for International Economics, 1974). See also G. Ragazzi, 'Theories of the Deter- minants of Direct Foreign Investment', *IMF Staff Papers*, 20 (1973), 471–98.

Despite the recent growth of European investment, the US remains the principal foreign investor in most countries because of the cumulative effect of its high level of investment throughout the post-war period. Table 1.2 shows that in 1968, 13.4 per cent

TABLE 1.2 Foreign ownership of UK manufacturing industry, 1968.

Nationality of firm	Net output (£m.)	Net output per head (£)	Average net output per enterprise (£m.)	Number of establishments per enterprise
United Kingdom	12,294.7	1,878	2.01	1.32
United States	1,479.6	2,772	3.03	2.28
Canada	111.8	3,043	5.32	2.52
Netherlands	108.9	2,132	4.94	4.91
Switzerland	87.6	2,404	2.74	2.72
France	56.8	2,481	2.36	1.96
Sweden	25.9	2,307	1.73	1.60
Australia	9.2	3,436	0.66	3.36
West Germany	7.3	1,884	0.38	1.16
Irish Republic	1.3	1,568	0.19	1.0
Denmark	0.7	2,122	0.14	1.2
South Africa	0.5	1,646	0.17	1.7
Other countries	5.8	1,657	0.34	1.35
Total non-UK	1,895.4	2,694	2.842	2.36

Source: UK Census of Production (1968), vol. 158, Summary Tables, Enterprise Analysis, Table 43.

of the net output of UK manufacturing industry was in the hands of foreign-controlled firms – and by far the largest stake, 78 per cent, was attributable to the US. The high foreign content of domestic production, and the predominance of US investment, is typical of other countries as well. The ranking of the remaining stakes in UK industry – illustrated diagramatically in Fig. 1.5 – is rather surprising, small countries such as Netherlands and Switzerland outperforming much larger countries such as France and West Germany.

It is not just the sources of foreign investment which are distinctive, but the countries and regions to which it is directed. Table 1.3 shows that a relatively low proportion of subsidiaries are established in less developed countries (LDCs). For colonial powers such as UK, Belgium, France, Netherlands and Portugal

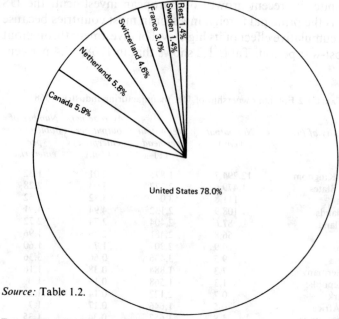

Source: Table 1.2.

FIG. 1.5 The distribution of foreign ownership in UK manufacturing industry by country of origin, 1968.

TABLE 1.3 Distribution of subsidiaries of MNEs between developed and less developed countries, by nationality of parent.

Nationality of parent	Percentage of subsidiaries located in less developed countries
United States	25.3
United Kingdom	31.8
Belgium–Luxembourg	30.3
France	40.3
West Germany	17.8
Netherlands	27.4
Switzerland	14.4
Sweden	16.6
Denmark	15.2
Italy	32.7
Norway	15.5
Austria	19.0
Spain	26.9
Portugal	50.0

Source: United Nations, Department of Economic and Social Affairs, *Multinational Corporations in World Development*, Appendix, Table 11.

the proportion of subsidiaries located in LDCs is about 30–40 per cent, while for non-colonial countries it is as low as 15 per cent. Moreover, within the developed countries a large proportion of foreign investment seems to be attracted to the most highly developed regions such as the coastal areas of Belgium, Netherlands and West Germany, and the south-east of England. It has therefore been argued that foreign direct investment tends to widen rather than reduce income disparities between nations by channelling resources into areas which are already highly developed, to the neglect of the less developed ones.

It seems clear that recent patterns of investment cannot be explained by the theory that capital-abundant countries invest in capital-scarce countries. Only the traditional flows of US investment to South America, UK investment to Africa, and US and UK investment to the Asia and Pacific region accord with this view. The post-war preference of US firms for investment in Europe, and the acceleration of intra-European investment and of European and Japanese investment in the US have to be explained by some other mechanism.

1.3   The size and international diversification of MNEs

It has been estimated that there are about 20,000 MNEs in the world economy, many of them quite small firms. Nevertheless one of the most remarkable features of multinationality is its relatively high incidence among very large firms. From the policy point of view the problems posed by multinationality are inextricably linked with problems of large size in general.

Table 1.4 shows the value added by the productive activities of some of the world's largest firms, compared to the equivalent measure – gross national product (GNP) – for a number of small or relatively poor countries; the countries shown are estimated to produce less than the companies ranked above them in the table. It can be seen that a giant utility such as American Telephone and Telegraph produces more than do the entire economies of countries such as Greece, Israel, Norway and Venezuela. More surprising, perhaps, is that manufacturing firms such as General Motors and Exxon (Esso), which are specialised in vehicles and consumer durables in the one case and oil in the other case, produce more than do the national economies of either Ireland, New Zealand or Pakistan.

TABLE 1.4 The estimated value products of the world's largest firms in 1973, ranked against the estimated gross national products of selected countries, and showing (a) the number of countries in which their subsidiaries are established and (b) the approximate percentage of their total production undertaken overseas.

Company	Country of registration	Value product ($'000m.)	(a)	(b)
American Telephone and Telegraph *Greece, Israel, Norway, Venezuela*	US	17.4	na	5
General Motors *Ireland, New Zealand, Pakistan*	US	8.1	21	24
Exxon (Esso)	US	5.7	25	81
Royal Dutch Shell group *Morocco, Kuwait*	Netherlands–Britain	5.4	43	70
Ford Motor	US	5.0	3C	36
ITT	US	4.2	40	60
Sears Roebuck	US	4.1	na	40
IBM	US	3.8	80	36
Unilever	Britain–Netherlands	3.8	31	70
Philips *Singapore*	Netherlands	3.7	29	67
General Electric	US	3.6	32	15
General Telephone and Electronics	US	3.1	na	15
Texaco	US	3.1	30	65
Siemens	West Germany	2.8	52	17
Chrysler *Ethiopia*	US	2.6	26	22
Mobil Oil	US	2.5	62	45
US Steel	US	2.3	na	60
ICI	Britain	2.3	46	42
Gulf Oil	US	2.3	61	75
Hitachi	Japan	2.2	na	0
Mitsubishi Heavy Industries	Japan	2.2	na	10
Volkswagen	West Germany	2.0	12	25
Standard Oil of California *Jordan, Luxembourg*	US	2.0	26	46

Source: Details of the firms are from *Fortune*, 1974, various issues, reporting on the 500 largest US industrial firms, the 200 largest US non-industrial firms, and the 300 largest non-US industrial firms for the financial year 1973. Value products are estimated from asset and employment data, assuming a 20 per cent return on assets, gross of depreciation, interest payments and tax, and assuming that employees are paid an average annual wage of $5000. Details of GNPs are from the *UN Statistical Yearbook* (1973), Table 182, updated using price and exchange-rate information from *International Financial Statistics*, November 1974, and assuming a 10 per cent real rate of growth in each country since the last year for which GNP data is available. Despite the obvious short-comings, it is believed that there is little danger that the value products of the firms have been overstated relative to the GNPs of the countries. Information in columns (a) and (b) is based on United Nations, Department of Economic and Social Affairs, *Multinational*

Clearly, if economic power confers political influence then the managements of these giant firms may have a greater impact on world relations than the governments of the countries in which they trade.

The threat to national interests from multinationality *per se* stems from the fact that many MNEs are potentially 'foot-loose' international investors. Government policy toward such firms has to be tempered by the realisation that in the face of undue restrictions, production – and in the long run, investment – can be switched very easily to subsidiaries in other parts of the world. A rough indication of how foot-loose a firm is in response to government policy is provided by its degree of international diversification. Two possible indices of international diversification are shown in the right-hand columns of Table 1.4: they are (*a*) the number of countries in which the firm's subsidiaries operate, and (*b*) an estimate of the percentage of the firm's sales accounted for by production abroad.

Column (*a*) shows that nearly all the large firms for which information is available operate in more than 20 countries, though some of the other large firms probably operate in less. The electrical firms IBM, Siemens and ITT operate in respectively 80, 52 and 40 countries, while the oil firms Mobil, Gulf and Shell operate in respectively 62, 61 and 43 countries. However, many overseas subsidiaries are concerned solely with marketing instead of production, and so are only very small economic units; the figures quoted may therefore overstate the economic significance of the firm's foreign operations. Nevertheless the statistics in column (*b*) suggest that any overstatement is relatively small.

It should be borne in mind that these remarks concern only a very limited number of very large firms, which are not necessarily representative of MNEs as a whole. Table 1.5 summarises information on a much larger population of firms, which includes medium-sized as well as large firms, and it exhibits on average a much lower degree of multinationality.

Corporations in World Development (New York, 1973), Appendix, Table 3, supplemented by various published and unpublished sources.

Note: Firms are ranked by value product; countries estimated to have a GNP somewhere between the value products of two successive firms are inset in the left-hand side of the table.

TABLE 1.5 Variations in international diversification of MNEs by nationality of parent, 1968–9.

Nationality of parent	Number of parents	Percentage of parents with affiliates in			
		1 country	*2–9 countries*	*10–19 countries*	*Over 20 countries*
United States	2468	50	38	9	3
United Kingdom	1692	43	48	6	3
Belgium–Luxembourg	253	58	37	4	1
France	538	39	51	8	2
West Germany	954	47	47	5	1
Netherlands	268	34	56	7	3
Switzerland	447	47	45	6	1
Sweden	255	36	51	9	3
Denmark	128	42	54	3	1
Italy	120	47.5	45	2.5	5

Source: United Nations, Department of Economic and Social Affairs, *Multinational Corporations in World Development*, Appendix, Table 4.

The host country's view of international diversification is given in Table 1.6. It shows for example that in the UK 92 per cent of all foreign-controlled subsidiaries are affiliated to parents operating in 12 or more other countries, and that 70 per cent

TABLE 1.6 International diversification of non-US MNEs in 1971, illustrated by the percentage of subsidiaries in the host country affiliated to (*a*) parents operating in 12 or more other countries, and (*b*) parents having more than half their employment abroad.

Host country	(*a*)	(*b*)
	Percentage of subsidiaries	
United States	86	56
Canada	86	35
United Kingdom	92	70
Belgium–Luxembourg	71	31
France	89	43
West Germany	92	50
Brazil	69	21
Mexico	79	28
Netherlands	80	35
Switzerland	82	49
Japan	94	43

Source: J. W. Vaupel and J. P. Curhan, *The World's Multinational Enterprises* (Geneva, 1974), Tables 25.1.1, 26.1.1.

are affiliated to parents which have more than half their employment abroad. This suggests that a high proportion of MNEs in UK industry are potentially foot-loose firms.

1.4   Distribution of MNEs by industry

There are a number of apparent regularities in the distribution of MNEs by industry.

Table 1.7 exhibits a breakdown by industry of the share of 300 large US-based MNEs in domestic production in eight selected countries. It shows that despite variations in US penetration between countries – ranging from 6 per cent in France to 52 per cent in Canada – there are just six out of the 14 industry groups in which US penetration is consistently high: chemicals, rubber, machinery (electrical and non-electrical), transport equipment, and instruments. These six industries may be loosely described as 'high-technology' industries, where research and development (R and D), the skills of highly trained labour, and the services of sophisticated plant and equipment all play a key role in boosting productive efficiency. The high participation rate of MNEs in these industries is not confined to US firms, although it is most apparent in the US case (further details are given in Chapter 4).

MNEs also tend to predominate in industries where output is concentrated in the hands of just a few producers. Table 1.8 exhibits a sample of 32 UK industries ranked by concentration and by foreign penetration. Concentration is measured by the proportion of domestic production accounted for by the five major producers, and foreign penetration by the proportion of domestic production accounted for by foreign-controlled firms; the industries are defined by fairly homogeneous product groups, so that the measure of concentration represents quite well the extent to which the industry departs from 'atomistic competition' as defined in economic theory. The ranking by concentration is very similar to the ranking by foreign penetration, suggesting that MNEs do indeed occur more frequently in highly concentrated industries. The only exceptions are copper, where concentration is high but foreign penetration low, and earth-moving equipment, where concentration is low but foreign penetration high.

A numerical measure of the degree of association between

TABLE 1.7 Percentage of output accounted for by 300 large US-based MNEs in the manufacturing industries of eight selected countries in 1970.

	United States	Canada	United Kingdom	Belgium–Luxembourg	France	West Germany	Brazil	Mexico
All manufacturing	35*	52*	16*	16*	6*	8*	18*	25*
Food	15*	26	10*	5	3	4*	3	8*
Paper	30*	39	5*	19*	8*	2	13	23*
Chemicals	57*	85	21*	48*	12*	7*	19*	20
Rubber	21	98	31*	82	6	11	48*	40
Metals	26*	29	10	6*	2	7*	12*	38*
Non-electrical machinery	37*	80*	21*	41*	14*	11*	34*	63*
Electrical machinery	58*	82	18*	43*	8*	6*	24*	52*
Transport equipment	77*	90*	27*	18	8	25*	65*	45
Textiles and apparel	9*	16*	1	10*	0	1	5*	3*
Lumber, wood and furniture	11*	50*	1	2	0	1*	1	2
Printing and publishing	4	12*	2*	1	1		1	1
Stone, clay and glass	28*	32*	6*	6*	9*	4*	9	26*
Instruments	66*	90*	56*	45*	20*	25*	na	na
Other manufacturing	29*	30*	30*	0	1	6	20*	64*

Source: US Tariff Commission Report on the Implications of Multinational Firms (Washington, 1973), ch. 7, Tables A43–56.

Note: An asterisk indicates that MNE penetration rose in the period 1966–70.

TABLE 1.8 Foreign penetration and concentration ratios for selected UK markets, 1968.

Product groups, ranked by degree of concentration	Five-firm concentration ratio (expressed as %)	Foreign penetration of production (%)	Ranking of markets by foreign penetration
Petroleum feedstocks	98.8	35	8
Rubber-processing chemicals	93.8	55	3
Cereal breakfast foods	93.5	73	1
Illuminating glassware	92.3	30	10=
Ball and other bearings	91.6	40	6=
Motor vehicles, complete	91.2	47	5
Blended whisky	91.0	6	21
Computers	90.5	32	9
Insulated power cables	90.5	5	23=
Copper	86.9	1	28=
Batteries and accumulators	84.1	6	22
Fats (excluding margarine)	82.6	21	14
Esters	82.5	14	17
Detergents	79.9	51	4
Cheese and processed cheese	77.7	30	10=
Preserved vegetables	66.7	40	6=
Belts, etc.	64.3	16	15=
Refractory bricks	63.9	4	25
Earth-moving equipment	63.0	65	2
Uncoated paper	54.8	1	28=
Nylon, rayon, glass fibre	51.9	2	27
Rubber and plastics machinery	50.6	7	20
Fabrics	47.2	5	23=
Gelatine and adhesives	46.1	29	12
Air-heating systems, complete	42.1	8	19
Plastic building materials	34.6	3	26
Needles, pins and fasteners	30.7	10	18
Meters	30.0	25	13
Overalls	27.4	0	30=
Metal-forming machine tools	26.9	16	15=
Canvas goods and sacks	24.9	0	30=
Builders' woodwork	23.0	0	30=

Source: A random sample taken from *UK Census of Production,* vol. 158, Summary Tables, Enterprise Analyses, Table 44, excluding industries which have been radically reorganised since 1968.

foreign penetration and concentration is provided by the Spearman rank-correlation coefficient, which ranges from −1 to +1. No association between two sets of ranks is indicated by a coefficient of zero, a perfect association by a coefficient of unity, and an exactly inverse relationship, where industries high on one scale are correspondingly low on the other, by a coefficient of minus one. The rankings shown in Table 1.8 have a Spearman coefficient of 0.59, which is highly significant,[2] and strongly suggests a systematic relation between foreign penetration and industrial concentration.

A similar statistical analysis may be performed using other industry characteristics. Recent data for the UK allow us to isolate at least five other interesting characteristics: the average industry wage rate, the average salary, the average ratio of staff to operatives, advertising expenditure as a percentage of net output, and royalty payments as a percentage of net output. With suitable qualifications these characteristics may be taken as indicating, respectively, the skill level of the labour force, the skill level of middle management and research workers, the degree of sophistication of the production process, the importance of marketing strategy, and the extent of reliance on brand names and patentable technical know-how.

The rank correlations between all pairs of the seven variables are summarised schematically in Fig. 1.6, which exhibits highly significant correlations by continuous lines linking the variables concerned, and other significant correlations by dotted lines; insignificant correlations are suppressed. The value of the Spearman coefficient is displayed next to the appropriate line. The figure shows that foreign penetration is the 'hub' of industry characteristics; industries with high foreign penetration are not only highly concentrated but also pay higher than average wages and salaries, have a higher than average ratio of staff to operatives, spend more than most on royalties and, to a lesser extent, advertise more.

The correlations above do not allow us to distinguish the industry characteristics which are directly related to foreign

---

[2] Under suitable statistical assumptions we can work out from the formula of the Spearman coefficient what its probability distribution will approximate to when a sample of measurements is taken on two independent variables, and thereby assess for any given sample the probability that if the two variables are independent we shall get a value of the coefficient equal to or larger than that actually obtained. If this probability is less than 5 per cent we reject the hypothesis that the variables are independent and accept the hypothesis that there is a systematic relation between them; we say that the value of the Spearman coefficient is *significantly different from zero* (or *significant*, for short). If the probability is less than 1 per cent we accept the hypothesis of a systematic relation with even greater confidence, and say that the value of the coefficient is *highly significant*.

FIG. 1.6 Schematic diagram of the association between foreign penetration and industry characteristics in a sample of UK manufacturing industries in 1968.

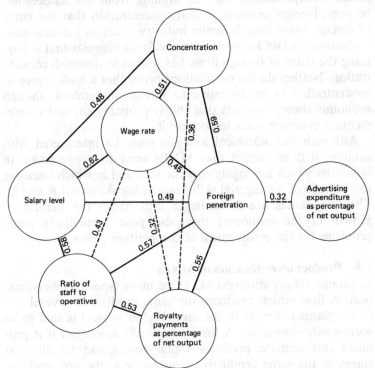

Source: Derived from *UK Census of Production* (1968), vol. 156, Summary Tables, Industry Analyses, Tables 3–5, and vol. 158, Summary Tables, Enterprise Analyses, Table 44.

Notes: The thick lines indicate associations for which the Spearman rank correlation coefficient is significant at the 1 per cent level, using the sample of industries exhibited in Table 1.8. The dotted lines indicate significant correlations at the 5 per cent level. The absence of a direct line from one circle to another indicates that the correlation between the variables concerned is not significantly different from zero.

penetration from those which are only indirectly related to it. For example, the association between the wage rate and foreign penetration may simply reflect a direct relationship between the wage rate and another variable, such as the salary level, which is in turn directly related to foreign penetration; this would lead to an apparent relationship between the wage rate and foreign penetration even if there were no underlying direct connection between the two. Nor do the correlations allow of casual interpretation, such as arguing from the association between foreign penetration and concentration that the entry of foreign firms into domestic industry tends to increase concentration; in fact supplementary evidence suggests that if anything the entry of foreign firms has tended to diminish concentration. Neither do the correlations prove that a high degree of concentration is an incentive to foreign investment, though economic theory suggests that this is probably so, and supplementary evidence tends to confirm it.

Although this statistical analysis must be interpreted with caution, it does suggest that MNEs tend to predominate in industries which are highly concentrated and in which intensive use is made of managerial skills, marketing skills and R and D. These industries are of strategic importance for the future growth of the economy; they also pose particularly acute problems for the enforcement of competition policy.

1.5   Product diversification of MNEs

Economic theory distinguishes three main types of diversification. A firm which produces the same product in several different plants (whether in the same region or not) is said to be *horizontally diversified*. A firm is *vertically diversified* if it produces intermediate products which correspond to different stages of the same productive sequence, e.g. the ore–steel–car body or hide–leather–shoe sequence. A firm is *conglomerately diversified* if it produces in more than one productive sequence. Any given firm may exhibit more than one type of diversification.

It is difficult to distinguish between types of diversification using available data. Casual empiricism suggests that horizontal diversification is very common, since a large majority of foreign subsidiaries produce broadly the same commodities as the parent, with minor modifications to suit local conditions or tastes. Case studies of selected industries – synthetic materials,[3] electronic components,[4] consumer durables,[5] etc. – tend to

---

[3] See G. C. Hufbauer, *Synthetic Materials and the Theory of International Trade* (London, 1965).
[4] See S. Hirsch, *Location of Industry and International Competitiveness* (Oxford, 1967).
[5] See L. T. Wells, 'Tests of a Product Cycle Model of International Trade', *Quarterly Journal of Economics*, 83 (1969), 152–62.

confirm the prevalence of horizontal diversification, particularly in the overseas operations of US-based firms.

The data presented in Table 1.9 suggest that other types of diversification are also important. The table shows that just

TABLE 1.9 Percentage distribution of the aggregate sales of foreign subsidiaries of 200 large non-US MNEs by the number of industries in which the firm manufactures abroad.

Number of industries	Percentage of sales
1–3	4
4–9	47
10–19	24
20 and over	24

Source: J. W. Vaupel and J. P. Curhan, *The World's Multinational Enterprises* (Geneva, 1974), Table 28.2.

under half the sales of the 200 largest non-US firms are accounted for by firms operating in ten or more industries. However, because of the fairly narrow definition of an industry (manufacturing is classified into 54 groups), firms diversified over less than ten industries may still be concentrated in a range of industries with broadly similar technologies or closely related product lines. Even so, it is clear that diversification over product groups is an important feature of the larger MNEs.

The relative importance of vertical and conglomerate types of diversification is difficult to measure. There is some evidence that the more multinational firms tend to be vertically diversified and the less multinational ones conglomerately diversified. Indirect support for this view is given in the first row of Table 1.10, which shows that 49 per cent of the world-wide exports of 300 large US-based MNEs were accounted for by intra-firm exports, i.e. exports of intermediate products from one part of the enterprise to another. Such a high proportion of intra-firm trade suggests that the typical subsidiary is part of an integrated process of production, drawing its inputs from and supplying its output to other divisions of the enterprise.

Given that MNEs are both vertically integrated and concentrated in high-technology industries it is interesting to discover whether these two features are associated, in the sense that vertical integration is most extensive in the high-technology

TABLE 1.10 Intra-firm trade of 300 large US-based MNEs by industry in 1970.

Industry	Intra-company of MNEs as a percentage of their total exports	Rank of percentage
All manufacturing	49	
Research-intensive industries		
Instruments	62	1
Transport equipment	61	2
Non-electrical machinery	52	3=
Electrical machinery	45	7
Chemicals	40	9
Rubber	50	5
Non-research-intensive industries		
Food	34	11
Paper	46	6
Metals	15	14
Textiles and apparel	52	3=
Lumber, wood and furniture	20	13
Printing and publishing	41	8
Stone, clay and glass	25	12
Other manufacturing	36	10

Source: US Tariff Commission Report, ch. 3, Table A14.

Note: Classification by research-intensity is based on the ratio of R and D expenditure to sales in the US.

field. Table 1.10 suggests that this is indeed so. The table classifies industries by research intensity, and shows the percentage of MNEs' world-wide exports accounted for by intra-firm exports, together with the ranking of industries by this percentage. It is clear that the percentage of intra-firm exports is on average higher in the research-intensive industries.

It is a characteristic of trade in research-intensive industries that it involves not just the exchange of intermediate products, as described above, but also substantial international remittances of management fees and royalty payments. The fact that MNEs are particularly active in these industries, suggests that as a result of their growth the percentage of international remittances of royalties and fees represented by intra-firm payments will have increased very considerably over recent years. Table 1.11, column 2, shows that for the US over the eleven-year period 1960–71 the percentage of intra-firm payments has risen by an average of just over 1 per cent per annum, from 62 per

TABLE 1.11 Gross receipts on royalties and fees accounts for US, 1960–71.

	(1)	(2)	(3)
Year	Total receipts ($m.)	Receipts of MNE parents from subsidiaries as a percentage of (1)	Percentage of MNE receipts from subsidiaries accounted for by royalties rather than fees
1960	650	62	na
1961	707	65	na
1962	836	69	na
1963	932	71	na
1964	1057	72	35
1965	1259	73	36
1966	1383	74	35
1967	1538	74	38
1968	1700	73	42
1969	1895	74	47
1970	2199	74	49
1971	2495	75	50

Source: US Tariff Commission Report, ch. 6, Table 7.

cent in 1960 to 75 per cent in 1971. Although very high, these figures actually understate the overall involvement of MNEs in international remittances of royalties and fees, since they ignore MNE receipts from foreign firms other than their subsidiaries; the total involvement of MNEs is probably nearer 90 per cent.[6] The right-hand column of the table indicates that the proportion of intra-firm remittances accounted for by royalties and licence fees rather than management fees has also increased significantly, from 35 per cent in 1964 to 50 per cent in 1971. Although the importance of intra-firm remittances of royalties and fees is on average lower in countries such as the UK, the trends noted above are still evident.

Intra-firm payments of this kind pose a serious problem for tax authorities, since it is very difficult for them to assess whether these payments are genuinely made in return for services rendered by the parent to the subsidiary, or are just a way of disguising the repatriation of profits, or worse still, of moving money balances around the world in response to speculative factors. It is often alleged that MNEs distort intra-firm payments so as to minimise their world-wide tax liabilities, to

[6] See *US Tariff Commission Report*, p. 600.

bypass exchange controls, and so on, but hard evidence on this point is (not surprisingly) difficult to obtain.

1.6 MNEs and their domestic competitors

So far we have focused on the distribution of MNEs across industries without considering whether within the same industry MNEs behave any differently from other firms. All the evidence suggests that within industries MNEs exhibit the same regularities as they do across industries, in particular they undertake more R and D than average, they have higher labour productivity, and employ a relatively high proportion of administrative personnel. These regularities are exhibited in Table 1.12 which shows that (*a*) without exception in US industries, MNEs undertake more R and D per unit of sales than do other firms, (*b*) the national industries in which MNEs have higher labour productivity than other firms outnumber those in which they do not by about four to one, and (*c*) the number of national industries in which MNEs have a higher ratio of staff to operatives than other firms outnumber those in which they do not by about two to one.

Table 1.13 shows that out of 48 research-intensive national industries in eight selected countries, US-based MNEs export more than do other firms in 24 cases, less than others in 21 cases, and about the same as others in one case; for the remaining two cases data are not available. However, in non-research-intensive industries MNE export performance is better than average in 39 out of 64 cases, worse than average in only 19 cases, and about the same in three cases; for the remaining three cases data are not available.

Thus in research-intensive industries, where their foreign penetration is high (cf. Table 1.8), MNE export performances are a little below average, while in other industries their performance tends to be above average. One possible explanation is that in the research-intensive industries, there are certain advantages for MNEs in producing close to the market, so that only a small proportion of their output is exported, while in non-research-intensive industries these advantages are out-weighed by the advantages of concentrating production so as to fully exploit the abundance of resources in certain locations, which then become export centres for the company's global operations.

TABLE 1.12 Comparison of US-based MNEs with other firms in the same industry – I. (a) Ratio of expenditure on R and D to sales for MNEs as a percentage of the value for other firms in the same US industry in 1966. (b) Labour productivity (sales per employee) for MNEs as a percentage of the value for other firms in the same industry. (c) An indicator of whether the ratio of staff to operatives for MNEs as a percentage of the value for other firms in the same industry is higher for MNEs, for selected countries, 1970.

Industry	(a)	United States	Canada	United Kingdom	Belgium–Luxembourg	France	West Germany	Brazil	Mexico
		(b), (c)							
All manufacturing	230	99*	140*	182*	132*	147*	134*	149*	158*
Food products	4970	92=	100	197*	98*	89*	101*	118*	211*
Paper and allied products	730	84*	102	202	97*	104*	83*	142*	166
Chemicals and allied products	520	69	120	126	204*	151*	157*	94*	146
Rubber	820	116*	129*	117*	167	128	128*	183*	115*
Primary and fabricated metals	128	92*	117*	106*	110=	98*	115*	153*	123*
Non-electrical machinery	300	93*	121*	173=	148*	201*	186*	169*	211*
Electrical machinery	110	96	140	100	126*	103	119=	121*	132*
Transport equipment	120	83*	153*	153	115*	111	125=	126*	203
Textiles and apparel	2520	121*	134	182*	143*	264	69	208*	194
Lumber, wood and furniture	∞	na[na]	111*	100	na[na]	na	na[na]	129[na]	115[na]
Printing and publishing	∞	139*	149*	85*	23*	64*	36*	208[na]	na[na]
Stone, clay and glass	1200	93*	119*	118*	159*	167*	117*	189[na]	124[na]
Instruments	410	109*	180	207	218	250	189	na[na]	na[na]
Other manufacturing	∞	201*	186*	633	186*	377	251	145*	83

Sources: R and D ratios derived from *US Tariff Commission Report*, Table 1, p. 556 and Tables A43–57, pp. 733–47. Sales per employee data based on Tables A66–80, pp. 756–70. Ratios of staff to operatives derived from Tables A66–97, pp. 756–87.

Notes: Asterisk indicates that the ratio of staff to operatives is higher from MNEs than for other firms, and = that the ratios are the same; na indicates satisfactory data is not available.

TABLE 1.13 Comparison of US-based MNEs with other firms in the same industry – II (for selected countries, 1970). (a) Percentage of exports accounted for by 300 large US-based MNEs in the manufacturing industries of eight countries. (b) An indicator of whether US-based MNEs export on average a higher proportion of their output than do other firms.

(a), (b)

Industry	United States	Canada	United Kingdom	Belgium–Luxembourg	France	West Germany	Brazil	Mexico
All manufacturing	68*	44	16=	13	10*	8=	28*	30*
Research-intensive industries								
Instruments	75*	100*	45	3	19	9	na	na
Transport equipment	104*	85	32	6	17*	22	40	100*
Non-electrical machinery	45*	34	19*	33	21*	7	100*	37*
Electrical machinery	69*	26	17*	26	7	7	28*	71*
Chemicals	61*	29	21*	41	8	5	100*	24*
Rubber	79*	42	18	41	8*	3	60*	100*
Non-research intensive industries								
Food	100*	25	13*	10*	7*	15*	6*	22*
Paper	54	30	7*	14	7*	4*	83*	0
Metals	75*	6	6*	5	1	3	3	15*
Textiles and apparel	26*	34*	0	14	0=	1=	3	7*
Lumber, wood and furniture	89*	34	9*	0=	1*	2*	3*	54*
Printing and publishing	44*	29*	8*	8*	4*	2	na	11*
Stone, clay and glass	76*	74*	13*	11*	10*	3	na	65*
Other manufacturing	36*	35*	2	1*	10*	7	na	11

Source: US Tariff Commission Report, ch. 3, Tables A25 and 27.

Notes: An asterisk indicates that US-based MNEs export on average a higher proportion of their output than do other firms. The data for MNEs and other firms are not always comparable, so that the percentage shown are only approximate. In particular, percentages in excess of 100 have been rounded down to 100.

Table 1.14 suggests that MNEs are more profitable than other firms in the same industry. Meaningful and accurate measures of profitability are difficult to obtain for any firm, and doubly so for subsidiaries of MNEs, since disguised repatriation of

TABLE 1.14 Comparison of MNEs with other firms in the same industry – III. Average rates of return earned by foreign and domestic firms in UK manufacturing industry in 1965 and 1969.

| Industry | Rate of return in | | | |
	1965		1969	
	UK firms	Foreign firms	UK firms	Foreign firms
Food, drink, and tobacco	10.8	12.3*	6.6	9.7*
Chemicals and allied products	9.2	17.2*	6.7	9.2*
Metal manufacture	8.6	6.5	6.4	11.1*
Mechanical engineering	7.2	13.1*		
Electrical engineering	9.8	10.3*	6.8	9.1*
Vehicles	11.8	10.9	6.2	7.8*
Other manufacturing	10.0	9.6*		

Source: J. H. Dunning, *United States Industry in Britain* (London, 1973), Table 2.4, p. 78.

Note: An asterisk indicates that rate of return of foreign firms exceeds that of UK firms in the same industry.

profits, differing accounting conventions, and so on, complicate matters very considerably. Bearing in mind these qualifications, Table 1.14 shows that the average rates of return[7] for foreign firms operating in UK manufacturing industry were consistently higher than for local firms in a majority of industry groups in 1965, and were higher in all industry groups in 1969.

1.7 National characteristics of MNEs

The picture which emerges from the statistics given above is of a very dynamic multinational sector of world business, concentrated in high-technology, high-skill industries, and within these industries investing more heavily than other firms in R and D and in labour skills. The MNEs have higher than average labour productivity and higher than average profits. Collectively they constitute the fastest-growing sector of world business

[7] The average rate of return is defined as profit, net of depreciation and tax, as a percentage of total assets net of accumulated depreciation and current liabilities.

and, were it not for them, much of the rapid post-war growth – of European and South American economies in particular – would almost certainly have been forfeited.

Generalisations, however, can be dangerous, and before concluding this introductory survey it must be pointed out while there are very broad similarities between individual MNEs, there are also important differences. These differences are mainly concerned with the nationality of the parent.

We have already seen that the nationality of the parent is associated with differences in the average size of subsidiaries within the host country (Table 1.2), in the average size of the enterprise world-wide (Table 1.4), in the distribution of subsidiaries by host country (Table 1.3) and the overall degree of international diversification (Table 1.5).

There are also important differences between MNEs with respect to their average research-intensity. Table 1.15 shows that MNEs based in West Germany and Netherlands are more highly concentrated in research-intensive industries than are those based in the US, Switzerland and France; these in turn are more concentrated in research-intensive industries than Belgian, British, Japanese and Canadian firms. These differences may in part be accounted for by the continuing predominance of the colonial and imperial raw-material ventures undertaken by certain nations in the inter-war period. However, the fact that the differences still exist after the post-war expansion of foreign direct investment suggests that there may be underlying differences in national attitudes to R and D, or to multinational operations in general.

The data summarised in Table 1.16 suggest that something of this kind is true. Four groups of parent nations are distinguished – US, Western Europe, Japan and others – and three types of enterprise: the international enterprise (INE) which is highly multinational, the transnational enterprise (TNE), which is only moderately multinational, and the uninational enterprise (UNE). The right-hand half of the table shows that while in the US and Western Europe INEs and TNEs are significantly more concentrated in research-intensive industries than are UNEs, in Japan there is no significant difference between the research-intensity of either INEs, TNEs or UNEs. Since the Japanese INEs and TNEs are almost as research-intensive as

TABLE 1.15 Percentage distribution of foreign subsidiaries by industry group for selected countries in 1971, showing industries classified by research-intensity

Industry	Nationality of parent								
	West Germany	Nether-lands	United States	Switzer-land	France	Belgium–Luxembourg	United Kingdom	Japan	Canada
Research-intensive industries									
Precision goods	3.3	2.9	2.0	1.6	1.1	1.6	0.6	0.2	0.0
Transport equipment	5.7	0.2	6.0	0.5	8.5	0.8	4.7	8.4	1.6
Non-electrical machinery	12.0	5.6	14.0	18.0	7.4	9.5	8.1	14.0	41.0
Electrical machinery	18.0	34.0	9.6	12.0	9.6	9.1	11.0	17.0	17.4
Chemicals	46.0	32.0	29.0	35.0	24.0	25.0	21.0	8.0	0.0
Rubber	2.1	0.2	3.0	0.8	3.5	0.0	2.4	2.7	0.0
Petroleum	1.2	10.0	5.5	0.3	9.6	6.3	3.4	0.2	0.0
Total percentage	88.3	84.9	69.1	68.2	63.7	52.3	51.2	50.5	50.0
Non-research-intensive industries									
Food	0.3	0.5	14.0	21.0	0.5	2.0	25.0	5.3	18.0
Primary metals	6.6	1.7	3.0	3.5	11.0	15.0	8.4	9.4	18.0
Textiles and apparel	1.1	3.2	2.7	5.1	2.1	6.7	4.1	28.0	0.0
Wood, paper and furniture	1.8	0.7	5.3	0.8	1.3	7.1	5.6	2.5	7.4
Other	2.4	8.0	6.2	1.1	21.0	17.0	5.2	4.1	5.9
Total number of subsidiaries	666	410	—	371	376	253	2160	438	188

Source: J. W. Vaupel and J. P. Curhan, *The World's Multinational Enterprises* (Geneva, 1974), Tables 8.1, 8.21.1.

Notes: US figures are for 1968. Countries are ranked from left to right by the percentage of foreign subsidiaries in research-intensive industries.

TABLE 1.16. 613 of the world's largest firms in 1971 classified by multinational status and research-intensity.

Country of registration	Percentage of value of sales accounted for by firms in research-intensive industries			
	INEs[2]	TNEs[3]	UNEs[4]	All firms
United States	54.6	31.2	28.2	48.0
Western Europe[5]	54.6	13.7	9.5	48.5
Japan	44.9	42.6	42.2	42.9
Other[6]	—	—	—	—
All countries	53.7	26.2	28.9	46.7

Source: J. E. S. Parker, *The Economics of Innovation* (London, 1974), condensed form.

Notes
(1) R- and D-intensive industries are aircraft, electrical engineering, scientific instruments, chemicals, petroleum and pharmaceuticals.
(2) INEs are companies having more than five producing affiliates in different countries, or more than 15 per cent of total group sales accounted for by foreign manufacturing activity.
(3) TNEs are companies which have more than two, and up to five foreign subsidiaries, each in different countries, or between 5 and 15 per cent of total group sales accounted for by foreign manufacturing activity.
(4) UNEs are companies which have two or less subsidiaries abroad, or derive less than 5 per cent of their sales from foreign production.
(5) Western European countries include United Kingdom, West Germany, France, Sweden, Netherlands, Italy, Switzerland, and Belgium.
(6) Other countries include Canada, Spain, Luxembourg, Australia, and South Africa.

their US and Western European counterparts, this suggests that Japanese firms tend in fact to be less multinational than others for a given level of research-intensity. It is possible to explain this by the relatively recent 'take-off' of Japanese high-technology industry which has prevented Japanese firms from expanding abroad as much as their US and Western European counterparts, but it may also reflect a national characteristic which predisposes Japanese firms to service foreign markets by exports rather than foreign production.[8] A possible explanation of this is the unusual system of Japanese labour relations – and the peculiarities of the Japanese business environment in general – which make it difficult for Japanese managers to adjust their methods to suit overseas production.

[8] For a recent comparison of US and Japanese patterns of foreign direct investment see K. Kojima, 'A Macroeconomic Approach to Foreign Direct Investment', *Hitotsubashi Journal of Economics*, 14 (1973), 1–21

1.8 Summary

The discussion above has highlighted a number of phenomena which require explanation.

Firstly, there is the dating of the 'take-off' of the multinationalisation of business to the immediate post-war period.

Secondly there is the fact that post-war international direct investments apparently do not conform to the theory that capital moves from capital-abundant countries to capital-scarce countries; the problem is not only that in certain cases capital flows in the 'wrong' direction, but that in several cases substantial amounts of capital in fact flow between two countries in both directions at once.

Thirdly, multinationality tends to be greater the larger the firm. To a certain extent, a firm operating in many countries naturally tends to be large, but this still leaves open the question of whether large firms in particular have a tendency to become multinational.

Fourthly, MNEs are concentrated in certain types of industry, characterised by high concentration and high research- and skill-intensity. Within these industries MNEs research more, employ more highly skilled labour, have a higher than average proportion of staff to operatives, and earn an above-average rate of return.

Fifthly, most MNEs are horizontally diversified, but relatively few are conglomerately diversified. Many of the very large MNEs are vertically diversified, particularly those in the research-intensive industries; these firms typically have high levels of intra-firm trade in intermediate goods and in know-how.

Finally, MNEs exhibit certain characteristics which are attributable to their nationality, e.g. the relatively high multinationality of British, Dutch and Swiss firms, and the low multinationality of even the most research-intensive Japanese firms.

An explanation of these phenomena is provided by the theory developed in the following chapter.

2 A Long-run Theory of the Multinational Enterprise

2.1 Introduction

It is little exaggeration to say that at present there is no established theory of the multinational enterprise. Previous economic and statistical studies of the MNE can be criticised on the grounds that they lack a comprehensive theoretical basis. But from another point of view the fault lies with the orthodox theories of production and trade because as presently formulated they are unable to explain or predict the post-war growth of MNEs. We shall argue that the growth of the MNE is one aspect of a radical change in business organisation which has outdated the orthodox theory of production.[1]

The two key assumptions of the orthodox theory are profit-maximisation and perfect competition (the latter implies that each commodity is traded between many small buyers and many small sellers in a market where knowledge of prices is perfect). Previous theories of the MNE have attempted to replace the orthodox theory either by relaxing profit-maximisation to allow for the pursuit of alternative managerial goals, or by relaxing perfect competition to allow for the exercise of monopoly or oligopoly power. The theory developed below endorses the second approach rather than the first, in that it depends on the assumption of profit-maximisation. However, it differs from the second approach in that it emphasises very general forms

[1] For a recent survey of the orthodox theory of production see G. C. Archibald (ed.), *Theory of the Firm*, Selected Readings (London, 1974). The theory of trade is based on the theory of production, see for example M. C. Kemp, *The Pure Theory of International Trade and Investment* (Englewood Cliffs, 1971).

of imperfect competition stemming from the costs of organising markets, and it concentrates on imperfections in intermediate-product markets rather than in final-product markets.

The outdating of the orthodox theory of production stems from the fact that the modern business sector carries out many activities apart from the routine production of goods and services: particularly important are marketing, R and D, the training of labour, the building of a management team, the procurement of finance and the management of financial assets, etc. All these business activities are interdependent and are connected by flows of intermediate products. The intermediate products are sometimes ordinary semi-processed materials passed on from one industry to another, but more often are types of knowledge and expertise, embodied in patents, human capital, etc. Efficient co-ordination of business activities requires a complete set of markets in the intermediate products. However, markets in certain intermediate products are difficult to organise, and it is our thesis that attempts to improve the organisation of these markets have led to a radical change in business organisation, one aspect of which is the growth of the MNE.

For the purposes of this book an MNE is defined as an enterprise which owns and controls activities in different countries. Our theory is based on three very simple postulates.

(1) Firms maximise profit in a world of imperfect markets.

(2) When markets in intermediate products are imperfect, there is an incentive to bypass them by creating internal markets. This involves bringing under common ownership and control the activities which are linked by the market.

(3) Internalisation of markets across national boundaries generates MNEs.

Section 2.2 analyses the internalisation of an intermediate-product market on the principle that internalisation is undertaken up to the margin where the benefits are equal to the costs. The analysis highlights the fact that when there are time-lags in business activities their co-ordination requires future markets as well as spot markets and that, when activities are geographically separated, communication costs are a major constraint on market efficiency. Four main groups of factors are relevant to the internalisation decision: (i) *Industry-specific factors* relating to the nature of the product and the structure of the external market, (ii) *Region-specific factors* relating to the geographical and social characteristics of the regions linked by the market, (iii) *Nation-specific factors* relating to the political and fiscal relations between the nations concerned, and (iv) *Firm-specific factors* which reflect the ability of the management to organise an internal market.

The main emphasis throughout this book is on the industry-specific factors. These factors suggest particularly strong reasons for internalising markets for intermediate products in certain multistage production processes, and for internalising markets in knowledge. The first type of internalisation generates the vertically integrated producer. The second type of internalisation leads to the integration of production, marketing and R

Fɪɢ. 2.1 Interdependency of firms' activities.

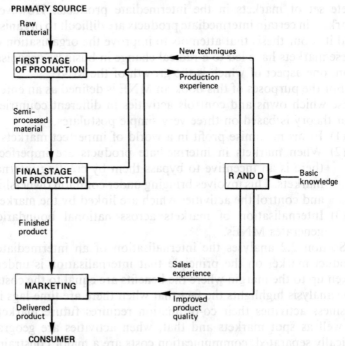

Notes: Successive stages of production are linked by flows of semi-processed materials. Production and marketing are linked by a flow of finished goods ready for distribution. Production and marketing on the one hand are linked to R and D on the other hand by two-way flows of information and expertise.

and D. A combination of these two types of integration is shown diagrammatically in Fig. 2.1.

The link between internalisation of markets and the internationalisation of the firm is explored in detail in section 2.3. It is argued that the location strategy of a vertically integrated firm is determined mainly by the interplay of comparative advantage, barriers to trade, and regional incentives to internalise; the firm will be multinational whenever these factors make it optimal to locate different stages of production in different nations.

The location strategy of a firm with integrated production, marketing and R and D has a characteristic form attributable to the fact that knowledge is a public good within the firm, and its transmission costs are normally low. This means that the exploitation of proprietary knowledge is logically an international operation. For similar reasons the search for relevant knowledge in a particular field is also an international operation. The firm thus operates an international intelligence system for the acquisition and collation of basic knowledge relevant to R and D, and for the exploitation of the commercially applicable knowledge generated by R and D. Unless either transport costs are very low, returns to scale at the plant level are high, or the comparative advantage of one location is very significant, the international acquisition and exploitation of knowledge will normally involve international production through a worldwide network of basically similar plants.

The integration of production, marketing and R and D can be used as the basis for a simple theory of the growth of the firm, which is expounded in section 2.4. The theory predicts that the more research-intensive firms will exhibit higher rates of growth and profitability, and will be more multinational than the average. These predictions are easily testable, given suitable data.

Section 2.5 presents a comparative dynamic analysis of the growth of multinationality, in terms of changing tastes and technologies acting on the incentive to internalise. It is argued that industry-specific factors have predominated in the growth of MNEs. The characteristics of MNEs are thus attributable not to multinationality *per se*, but to the factors which govern internalisation in the industries in which they operate.

Prior to the Second World War the major factor in the emergence of the MNE appears to have been the growth in the demand for primary products, and the difficulties of organising efficient external markets for them. Post-war, the increased demand for knowledge-based products and the increasing efficiency and scale-economies of knowledge production together with the difficulties of organising a market in knowledge, have constituted the major incentive to the growth of MNEs. In both periods a secondary influence has been the steady reduction in communication costs, and the increasing scope for tax reduction through transfer pricing.

2.2   The economics of internalising a market[2]

The theory presented in this chapter views the MNE as a special case of a multiplant firm, bringing under common ownership and control several interdependent activities linked by flows of intermediate products (cf. Fig. 2.1). As a preliminary, this section discusses the fundamental question in the theory of the multiplant firm, namely, why should interdependent activities by co-ordinated internally by the management of a firm rather than externally by market forces?

It is well known to economists that under certain conditions (such as non-increasing returns to scale), the co-ordination of interdependent activities by a complete set of perfectly competitive markets cannot be improved upon.[3] An important corollary of this is that there is no advantage in replacing a *perfect* system of markets by a centrally administered control system. Thus the incentive for internal co-ordination of activities by a firm does not rest on the advantages of centralisation *per se*. This view is reinforced by the fact that many firms, particularly the larger ones, operate a decentralised control system which has a close affinity to a market. In fact, it is a consequence of the result above that a necessary condition for an internal market to be

[2] The discussion below owes much to the classic analyses by R. H. Coase, 'The Nature of the Firm', *Economica*, 4 (1937), 386–405; N. Kaldor, 'The Equilibrium of the Firm', *Economic Journal*, 44 (1934), 60–76; and E. T. Penrose, *The Theory of the Growth of the Firm* (Oxford, 1961).

[3] A *complete set* of markets implies that there are no externalities, i.e. there are no unpriced flows of intermediate products between the activities; *perfect competition* implies that all firms are price-takers, and have perfect knowledge of the prices ruling in the markets.

more efficient than an external one is that the external market is imperfect.

The benefits of internalisation stem from the avoidance of imperfections in the external market, but there are also certain costs of internalisation which may offset the potential benefits. The optimal scale of the firm is set at the margin where the costs and benefits of further internalisation are equalised. The factors which govern this margin govern the scale of the firm. The following paragraphs consider in turn the factors which govern internalisation.

There are at least five types of market imperfection which generate significant benefits to internalisation.

Firstly, the interdependent activities linked by the market may involve significant time-lags, but the futures markets required for their co-ordination may be missing. When the activities involve significant time-lags between initiation and completion, co-ordination by market forces requires not only competitive spot markets, but competitive futures markets as well. In such cases a spectrum of marketable short- and long-term contracts is required to provide buyers and sellers with the price signals necessary to co-ordinate both short-term production schedules and long-term investment programmes. Spot markets are adequate for this purpose only in the steady state. When futures markets are lacking there is a strong incentive for firms to create their own internal futures markets by bringing the interdependent activities under common control.

Secondly, efficient exploitation of market power over an intermediate product may require discriminatory pricing of a kind which is not feasible in an external market; the mono-polist (or monopsonist) then has an incentive to integrate forward (or backward), so that he can implement the appropriate system of price discrimination in an internal market. For ex-ample, in the absence of discrimination a monopoly of a factor input may be exploited only by charging a uniformly high price which encourages substitution against the input. A discrimina-tory tariff based on the derived demand curve for the factor would more or less maintain the *average* price of the factor while removing entirely the incentive to substitute against it. It would therefore increase the monopolist's profit without reducing that of his customers. It follows that when discriminatory pricing in an external market is impracticable, internalisation of the market through merger of the firms concerned will potentially increase their combined profits by facilitating discriminatory pricing.

The third type of imperfection is where a bilateral concentration of market power leads to an indeterminate or unstable bargaining situation. The cost to each firm of the sanctions imposed against it by the other as part of the bargaining process, and the uncertainty stemming from the threat of such action, are best avoided either by agreement on a long-term contract binding the two parties, or a more permanent arrangement brought about through merger or takeover.

The fourth type of imperfection occurs when there is inequality between buyer and seller with respect to knowledge of the nature or value of the product. If the seller of an intermediate product is better informed than the buyer, but for one reason or another is unable to convince the buyer that the price requested is reasonable, then the seller has an incentive to shoulder the buyer's risk, either by taking over the buyer, or setting up in competition with him. 'Buyer uncertainty' may therefore encourage forward integration.

A special case of buyer uncertainty occurs in the marketing of public goods. A public good is one which can be sold many times over, because the supply to one person does not reduce the supply available to others. However, the value of a public good to the purchaser may depend on the number of other people also supplied. Since the marginal cost of an additional sale of the public good is zero, the purchaser has to rely on the seller's good faith that the supply of the good will be limited, and that it will not be sold to others at a lower price. If convincing safeguards cannot be provided then 'buyer's risk' will be high. In the case of an intermediate public good the logical solution is for the seller to assume the buyer's risk through forward integration into the buyers' industry.

The final type of imperfection has a specifically international aspect. It stems from government interventions in international markets, through *ad valorem* tariffs or restrictions on capital movements, and from discrepancies between countries in rates of income and profit taxation. Each of these interventions depends either directly or indirectly on, amongst other things, the valuation of internationally traded intermediate goods. In external markets prices are usually published, and so cannot easily be misquoted when the firm reports its liability for tax. However, in internal markets no such publicity exists, and imputed prices of intermediate goods are constrained only by the need for consistency in divisional accounting and by what the Customs and tax authorities will tolerate.

The discussion above suggests that there are certain markets in which the incentive to internalise is particularly strong. The strongest case of all concerns the markets for various types of knowledge.

Firstly, the production of knowledge through R and D, and its implementation in new processes or products, are lengthy projects which require detailed long-term appraisal and careful short-term synchronisation. In the absence of futures markets, effective planning requires internalisation of the market.

Secondly, knowledge is a 'natural monopoly' – at least for a limited period of time – and is best exploited through discriminatory pricing of some kind. Licensing systems cannot usually be designed to satisfy the discriminatory criteria, so that internalisation is again appropriate.

Thirdly, the prospective purchasers of knowledge are in many cases monopsonists, having control of local markets through ownership of distributive outlets etc. Since the proprietor of the knowledge is effectively a monopolist, there is a bilateral concentration of market power. The bargaining conflict may require some form of joint ownership to resolve it.

Fourthly, buyer uncertainty is almost inevitable whenever unpatentable or unregisterable knowledge is being marketed. To a certain extent it is possible to divulge information about knowledge – such as its commercial applications – without divulging the knowledge itself, but there are limits to the extent this can be done without giving away sufficient clues for the potential purchaser to discover the knowledge for himself. Once this occurs, of course, the value of the knowledge to the seller is eliminated. It is therefore essential that some buyer uncertainty is preserved, which means that inevitably the buyer is willing to pay less than the seller could afford to give were he in the same position. There is thus a strong incentive for the seller to assume the buyer's risk by internalising the knowledge and integrating forward into the buyer's industry.

This incentive is reinforced by the fact that knowledge is a public good. The demand for any type of knowledge – whether patented, or registered, or not – is likely to be retarded by uncertainty as to whether or not 'sole rights' to exploit the knowledge are safeguarded. For to maximise the rent from knowledge it is essential to preserve the element of natural monopoly. Sometimes licensing systems are devised which partition the world market on an agreed basis between the licensees, giving each a local monopoly. However, the costs of policing such systems, and the risks that they violate restrictive practices legislation, will encourage firms to exploit the knowledge themselves, or acquire by takeover the potential licensees.

Finally, because flows of knowledge are so difficult to value, they provide an excellent basis for transfer pricing.

Other markets where internalisation is likely to be advantageous are perishable agricultural products, intermediate products in capital-intensive manufacturing processes, and raw materials whose deposits are geographically concentrated.

Perishable agricultural products have a relatively volatile and unpredictable supply, compounded by short-run inelasticities in both supply and demand. This means that for the co-ordination of production, processing and distribution, short-term futures markets are essential. For standardised products where buyer uncertainty is low, futures markets are easily organised, but in other cases they need to be created by internalisation of the market.

Long-term futures markets are essential for the organisation of capital-intensive multistage production processes. When capital goods have a long life and few alternative uses it is important to appraise the prospective returns from the asset correctly, and to co-ordinate capacity expansions at the various stages of production, so that investment at one stage is not vitiated by bottlenecks at some other stage. In the absence of long-term futures markets, the most effective method of forward planning is to bring the various stages of production under common control.

Raw materials which are geographically concentrated are a classic case in which a monopoly of a key resource is liable to occur. In the absence of discriminatory pricing, manufacturers will have to purchase the resource at a uniform price above its marginal cost, which will encourage substitution away from the method of production which is optimal in terms of real resource costs. This will restrict use of the resource and reduce the actual profit earned by the monopolist below the potential profit available through discriminatory pricing. Internalisation of the market, by permitting discriminatory pricing, will restore the efficient method of production and increase the total profits from ownership and use of the resource.

Against the benefits of internalisation must be set the costs. It can be argued that under some circumstances an internal market will have higher resource costs and higher communication costs than a corresponding external market, and will be more prone to political interference.

The argument for higher resource costs assumes that internalisation normally involves splitting up a single external market into a number of separate internal markets. To take an extreme case, if there were a perfectly competitive market linking two activities then at plant level each activity would be operated at its optimal scale quite independently of the scale at which the other activity was operated. But once the market is split up and internalised within a number of distinct firms, the scale at which each activity operates has to be adjusted to the scale of the other activities within the firm. When different activities have different optimal scales, average costs are minimised only when the firm operates on a scale equal to the lowest common denominator of the optimal scales, thereby having an integer number of plants of optimal scale devoted to each activity. If such a scale of operations is not attained then the internalisation of markets distorts the scale of at least some activities, and hence reduces economic efficiency below what it would be under perfectly competitive external markets.

However, the difficulties can be reduced by only partially internalising the markets, so that at each stage a plant may dispose of excess output on the open market, or buy in additional inputs from outside the firm. In this case internal markets and external markets may exist side by side, with only a small loss of efficiency on account of internalisation. We conclude that the resource costs attributable to fragmentation of the market are unlikely to be a significant influence on the internalisation decision.

There are several reasons for believing that communication costs in an internal market will be much greater than in an external market.

Firstly, there will normally be a much greater flow of accounting and control information in an internal market, because a major reason for internalisation is that the information supplied by the external market is inadequate for rational decision-taking.

Secondly, if the market is fragmented then overheads will tend to be higher if each internal market has its own communication system. On the other hand, if the markets share the same system then there may be a problem of confidentiality – one firm may be able to profit by 'listening in' to the other firms' communications.

Finally, there is the problem of checking the accuracy of information supplied to the market, and ensuring that relevant information is not concealed. This is particularly important in an internal market, since the activities normally have a common owner, who has to ensure the accountability of the local managements involved. Ordinary transmissions of information can normally be handled by post and telecommunications, but checks usually require on-the-spot inspection, which can be relatively expensive if long-distance personal transportation is involved.

These three factors – the increased flow of information, the requirements of confidentiality and the importance of checking information through relatively expensive on-the-spot visits – all contribute to the increased cost of communication within an internalised market.

It can be argued that the additional communication costs make the internalisation decision dependent on the distances between the regions linked by the market, and on dissimilarities between them in language and social and economic environment. Consider the four stages of communication: encoding, transmitting, decoding and checking (Fig. 2.2). The personnel responsible for encoding and decoding must have similar backgrounds or operate in a similar environment, otherwise misunderstandings will arise because the implicit assumptions of

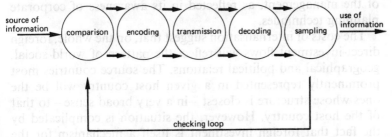

FIG. 2.2 Stages in the communication of information.

Note: Encoding involves putting information into communicable form – a document, letter, telegram, telephone message, etc.; *transmission* involves the movement across space of the embodied information; *decoding* involves interpreting the information in the light of background knowledge, while *checking* involves sampling the information and comparing it with an independent assessment of the facts.

the decoder will differ from those of the encoder. Misunderstandings can be avoided only by additional expenditure on checking. Either way, communication costs will vary with the economic, social and linguistic dissimilarities between the regions. Transmission costs are partly accounted for by the terminal costs of the system, but there are other significant costs which are dependent on the distances involved. Thus the additional communication costs of an internal market will also depend on geographical factors such as distance.

There is one cost of internalisation which is specifically international, and stems from the political problems associated with foreign ownership and control. The major problems are discrimination against foreign firms, through government patronage of indigenous producers, etc., and the threat of expropriation. These factors suggest that the net benefits of internalisation will be greater the more stable are political relations between the nations concerned, and the lower the strategic value attached to the industry by the host nation.

Finally, it must be recognised that the net benefits of internalisation depend on the ability of the management to organise an internal market, and to cope effectively with the problems of multiplant and multicurrency corporate accounting. The ability to do so will normally depend on the professionalisation of the management, as reflected in its awareness of corporate planning techniques.

The costs of internalisation suggest that, on the whole, foreign direct-investment flows will reflect the pattern of world social, geographical and political relations. The source countries most prominently represented in a given host country will be the ones whose structure is closest – in a very broad sense – to that of the host country. However, the situation is complicated by the fact that foreign investment is itself a mechanism for the transfer of social attitudes and social structures, so that similarities between nations not only influence, but are influenced by, foreign investment.

The discussion above may be summarised as follows. A market in an intermediate good will be internalised if and only if the benefits outweigh the cost. There are five main types of benefit, four of which – creation of internal futures markets, imposition of a discriminatory pricing system, avoidance of the costs of bilateral bargaining, and elimination of buyer uncertainty – depend mainly on the nature of the product and the structure of the external market. The fifth type of benefit is the ability to minimise the impact of government interventions through transfer pricing; the exploitation of transfer pricing depends not only on the nature of the product and the structure of the external market, but also on the characteristics of the fiscal systems in the various regions linked by the market. There are several main types of cost. The first is the resource cost of fragmentation of the market, which depends on the relation between the optimal scales of the activities linked by the market. The second is probably of greater importance: the additional communication cost attributable to internalisation. This cost is greater, the greater the geographical distance between the regions linked by the market, and the greater the 'social distance', i.e. the dissimilarities in language and the social and business environment. The third is the cost of political discrimination against foreign-owned firms, which will tend to be greater the more unstable are political relations between the nations concerned. The fourth is the administrative cost of the internal market, which depends largely on the professionalism of the management.

The conclusion is therefore that the incentive to internalise depends on the interplay of (i) industry-specific factors, namely the nature of the product, the structure of the external market and the relation between the optimal scales of the activities linked by the market, (ii) region-specific factors, namely the geographical and 'social' distance between the regions involved, (iii) nation-specific factors, namely the political and fiscal relations between the nations involved, and finally, (iv) firm-specific factors such as the degree of professionalisation of management.

2.3 Internalisation and the internationalisation of the firm

The link between the internalisation of markets and the existence of MNEs is very simple: an MNE is created whenever markets are internalised across national boundaries.

For example, vertical integration of production will give rise to MNEs because different stages of production require different combinations of factors and are therefore best carried out in different countries, according to factor availability and the law of comparative advantage.

There is a special reason for believing that internalisation of the knowledge market will generate a high degree of multinationality among firms. Because knowledge is a public good which is easily transmitted across national boundaries, its exploitation is logically an international operation; thus unless comparative advantage or other factors restrict production to a single country, internalisation of knowledge will require each firm to operate a network of plants on a world-wide basis.

The extent to which internalisation of markets implies internationalisation of the firm is examined in more detail below. The analysis is developed in two stages: the first stage presents an orthodox theory of location which ignores the factors relevant to internalisation; the second examines to what extent (if any) internalisation interacts with and modifies location strategy.

In the first stage of the analysis we consider in turn two main types of internalisation, namely vertical integration of a multistage production process, and the integration of production, marketing and R and D.

A schematic diagram of a multistage production process is given in Fig. 2.3: production involves a sequence of distinct activities connected by the transport of semi-processed materials.

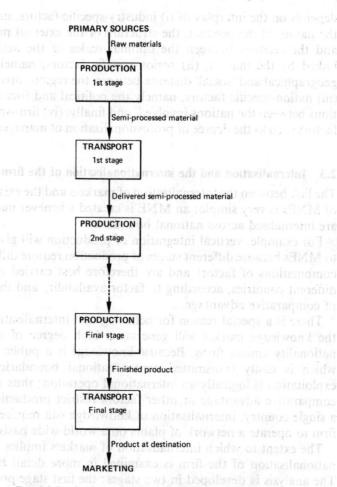

PRIMARY SOURCES
Raw materials

PRODUCTION
1st stage

Semi-processed material

TRANSPORT
1st stage

Delivered semi-processed material

PRODUCTION
2nd stage

PRODUCTION
Final stage

Finished product

TRANSPORT
Final stage

Product at destination

MARKETING

FIG. 2.3 Production as an integrated sequence of activities.

Note: The schematic diagram represents a multistage production process of a type common in manufacturing, assembly and construction. Division of labour resolves the production process into a sequence of activities which are technologically independent and can be carried out at different locations.

It is assumed that the choice of location is confined to a fixed number of regions. Both production and transport activities require non-tradeable inputs (mainly types of labour) whose prices vary between locations, and tradeable inputs (mainly the services of various types of durable good) whose prices are internationally uniform.[4] (Transport has access to all non-tradeable inputs available *en route*.) The technology of production is the same everywhere,[5] while the technology of transport between two locations depends on distance and on the geographical features of the region between them. We assume to begin with that the technologies exhibit constant returns to scale,[6] and that the firm is a price-taker in all factor markets.

Given the destination of the finished product, the optimal location of each constituent activity may be determined by a two-stage analysis. The first stage is the evaluation of the regional production costs and interregional transport costs for each activity, and the second is the minimisation of the overall average cost of production.

The first stage is simplified by the fact that when the firm is a price-taker in factor markets, constant returns to scale implies constant unit costs. Marginal analysis shows that when least-cost techniques are chosen, the regional variation in production costs is governed by regional differentials in the prices of non-tradeable inputs, the relative prices of tradeable inputs and the elasticities of substitution between pairs of non-tradeables and between non-tradeables and tradeables (but not between pairs of tradeables). Variations in transport costs depend on these factors and also on distances and the geographical features of the regions concerned.

Given the vector of regional unit costs for each stage of production and the matrix of interregional transport costs for each type of semi-processed material, the minimisation of overall unit cost becomes a dynamic programming problem of the type illustrated in Fig. 2.4. The problem is easily solved to obtain an optimal location strategy which reflects the interplay

---

[4] Tradeable inputs have negligible transport costs, non-tradeable inputs do not.

[5] Thus for example all differences in resource endowments are accounted for by including the resource as an argument in the production function.

[6] A case can be made both for increasing returns to scale on technological grounds, and for decreasing returns to scale because the quality of inputs declines with scale. We assume that these influences are negligible, or they cancel one another out.

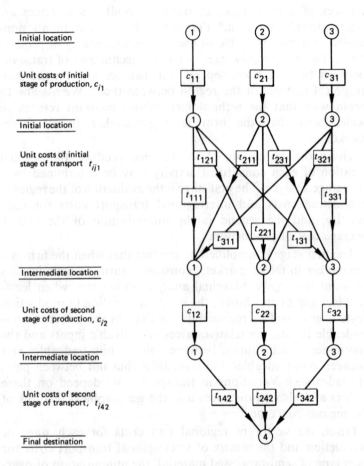

FIG. 2.4 Schematic diagram of a dynamic programming problem for a two-stage production process with a choice of three locations.

Note: The problem is to find the route from the top line to the bottom which scores the lowest total. Normally $t_{ijk} = t_{jik}$ and $t_{ijk} = 0$ if $i = j$ (k denotes the stage).

of production and transport costs at the various stages of production.

When there are several destinations to be serviced the analysis may be repeated for each of the destinations independently, and then aggregated to obtain an optimal pattern of trade.

A particularly simple location problem is illustrated graphically in Fig. 2.5. There are two regions A and B; both are potential markets and possible locations for production. Production requires two inputs; one (the numeraire) is tradeable, the other is not. The production function exhibits constant returns to

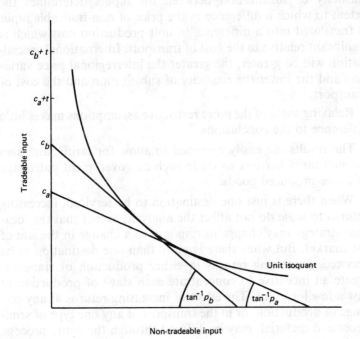

FIG. 2.5 Determination of the optimal trade strategy for two regions, A and B.

Notes
c denotes unit production cost
t denotes unit transport cost
p denotes the price of the non-tradeable input
Subscripts refer to the region.

Solution
Since $c_a < c_b + t$, A's market is serviced by domestic production
Since $c_b < c_a + t$, B's market is also serviced by domestic production
Thus there is no trade.

scale, and so is uniquely characteristic by the unit isoquant. The choice of technique for each region is determined by the point of tangency with the relevant isocost line, whose slope measures the price of the non-tradeable input, and whose intercept on the numeraire axis measures the unit cost of production. Since transport in either direction has access to non-tradeable inputs from both regions, *ceteris paribus* transport costs from A to B will be the same as from B to A. The figure shows how the elasticity of substitution between the inputs determines the extent to which a difference in the price of non-tradeable input is translated into a difference in unit production cost which is significant relative to the cost of transport. International specialisation will be greater, the greater the interregional price variation and the lower the elasticity of substitution and the cost of transport.

Relaxing some of the more restrictive assumptions makes little difference to the conclusions.

The results are easily extended to allow for tariffs, and also for non-tariff barriers to trade such as government patronage of home-produced goods.

When there is just one destination to be serviced, increasing returns to scale do not affect the analysis, except that the location strategy may change in response to a change in the size of the market. But when there is more than one destination to be serviced, increasing returns in either production or transport create an incentive to concentrate each stage of production at just a few locations. The effect of increasing returns at any one stage of production, or in the transport of any one type of semi-processed material, may be diffused through the entire process, leading to the relocation of plants involved in quite remote stages of production, and the reorganisation of the entire network of trade.

Relaxation of the assumption that the firm is a price-taker in factor markets complicates the analysis without introducing any new points of principle. Provided that the firm imputes a price to the input equal to its marginal cost, the firm's location strategy will be broadly similar to what it would be were the input purchased competitively at the imputed price, the only difference being that the imputed price of the input will tend to vary with the quantity used.

The location strategy of a firm which integrates production, marketing and R and D is highly complex, and only an outline can be presented here. An essential preliminary is to clarify the nature of marketing and R and D activities.

Marketing has three main constituent activities: stockholding, distribution and advertising (Fig. 2.6). In this chapter, only the

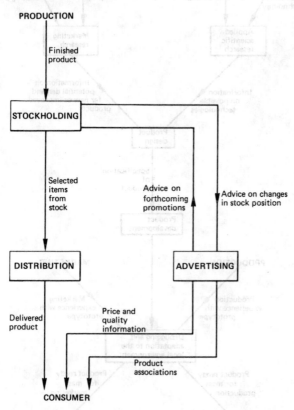

FIG. 2.6 Marketing as an integrated set of activities.

purely routine aspects of advertising are regarded as marketing activities; innovative aspects such as the design of new advertising campaigns are classified as R and D.

Our concept of R and D is very broad; it includes not only technical R and D but also marketing-oriented R and D. The inputs to R and D are highly skilled labour, sophisticated durable equipment and information obtained from the scientific

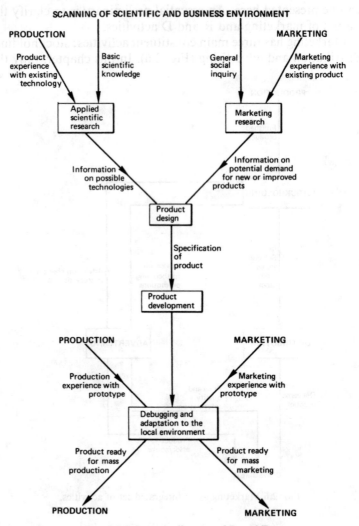

FIG. 2.7 Schematic diagram of R and D.

Notes

Applied scientific research may be directed either to the discovery of new technologies based on improved understanding of physical, chemical and biological processes, or to developing new managerial techniques – OR, O and M, etc. – relevant to processes under the firm's control.

Marketing research involves analysis of potential demand by region, social class, income group, etc., and the discovery of consumer's attribute-preferences for various types of product.

and business environment. R and D itself is a complex of inter-related activities connected by information flows: a typical R and D organisation is illustrated schematically in Fig. 2.7 and elaborated in the accompanying notes. The outputs of R and D are new or improved products, and new or more efficient processes of production. The latter may be embodied in either durable equipment or managerial methods.

The location of marketing activities is relatively straight-forward. Distribution and routine advertising are almost in-evitably located in the market, since they both involve direct communication with the consumer. The location of stockhold-ing is influenced by the fact that (i) the ratio of stock to sales required to maintain a given quality of service to the customer (e.g. immediate delivery from stock) almost certainly declines (at a reducing rate) as warehouse turnover increases, and (ii) the technology of warehouse design favours the larger ware-house (e.g. the ratio of cubic capacity to surface area increases with size). These factors encourage concentration of stock-holding at just one location. But against them must be set the additional costs of distributing to the consumer from a location remote from the market. The interplay of inventory and dis-tribution costs will tend to make local stockholding optimal for any volume of sales above a critical level (see Fig. 2.8).

Communication costs play the same role in the location of R and D as do transport costs in the location of production. In the absence of communication costs all R and D activities would be located where non-tradeable inputs, notably skilled labour, were cheapest. Assuming limited international mobility of skilled technicians, scientists and engineers, this could imply

---

Efficient *product design* involves combining attributes to maximise the potential market for a given production cost.

Product development is the engineering work which goes into constructing a prototype product to meet the design specification. It requires careful manage-ment to avoid wastage of time, materials and effort in the development process.

Debugging and adaptation of the product is the conversion of a prototype into a mass-produced product adapted to the needs of a local market and to the supply conditions in the optimal location for production. It involves trial marketing and production runs, followed by experimental modifications which, through careful monitoring, provide the experience necessary to standardise the product and the method of production. This final stage is essentially one of 'learning by doing'.

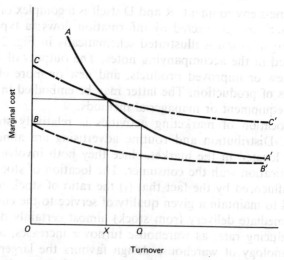

FIG. 2.8 Determination of the optimal location of inventory.

Notes

The distance OQ measures the initial turnover at the best existing foreign stock location

AA' is the marginal-cost curve of stockholding at any given location

BB' is the curve AA' displaced to the left by an amount OQ

CC' is the curve BB' displaced vertically by the increment in the marginal distribution cost attributable to the use of a foreign stock location rather than a local one

The distance OX measures the volume of sales above which stocks are located domestically

The figure assumes that the quality of service to the customer is fixed

the location of R and D in countries where educational facilities are most highly developed.

The impact of communication costs on the location of R and D is difficult to analyse because of the complexity of the information flows involved. The initial stages of R and D – applied scientific research and marketing research – require inputs of information from basic research institutions such as universities, and from trade associations, retail outlets, governments, etc. The firm has the option of acquiring this information at the earliest available opportunity from contacts and 'inside' sources, or waiting until the information has been published. The first strategy will almost certainly involve higher communication costs, due for example to the greater need for secrecy, and the consequent emphasis on personal contact, but it has the advantage of conferring a temporary monopoly in the commercial exploitation of the knowledge concerned. Generally speaking, the greater the reliance on inside knowledge, the greater the communication costs and the greater the incentive to locate R and D near to the source of information.

The intermediate stages of R and D – product design and development – normally require large-scale teamwork. The need for constant communication between team members suggests considerable advantages in centralising these activities at a single location.

The final stages of R and D – the debugging of new products and processes, and their adaptation to local conditions – require extensive two-way flows of information with the production and marketing divisions; there is thus a strong incentive to locate the final stages of R and D close to the major production centres and markets.

The remarks above suggest that while both the initial and final stages of R and D should be decentralised, the intermediate stages should not. The optimal location strategy appears to be to locate the initial stages of R and D close to the major sources of technical and marketing information, to distribute the final stages among the major production centres and markets, and to centralise the intermediate stages somewhere where skilled labour is cheap, but not too far away either from the major information sources or from the major production centres and markets.

Of the factors relevant to the internalisation of markets, as described in section 2.2, only two are liable to modify location strategy significantly.

The first is the incentive to minimise the impact of government intervention through transfer pricing. For example, when income and profit taxes differ internationally, overall tax liability is minimised by imputing the maximum possible mark-up to operations in the lowest-tax country (even though this normally involves higher tax burdens in other countries); full implementation of this policy may involve a complete change of location strategy to include a low-tax country in the firm's operations.

The second factor is the increased flow of accounting and control information in an internal market, and the consequently higher communication costs. The fact that communication costs increase with geographical and social distance tends to discourage the location of internally co-ordinated activities in very distant countries or regions.

2.4 Internalisation of knowledge: its implications for the growth and profitability of the MNE

If the MNE has evolved largely in response to incentives to internalise then it is possible that many of the characteristics of MNEs are attributable not to multinationality *per se* but to the factors which govern internalisation. In particular it can be argued that the internalisation of knowledge and the consequent integration of production and marketing with R and D generates a characteristic pattern of growth and profitability over the life of the firm.

It is convenient to distinguish two stages in the life of the research-intensive firm.

The first stage is one of aggressive expansion based on either the pursuit of a new avenue of research, generating a continual stream of new products or processes, or the continual improvement of existing products and processes. Internalisation of the knowledge generated by R and D implies that production and marketing must be expanded continually at a rate sufficient to absorb entirely within the firm the new products and new technologies generated by R and D. It is easily established that if production and marketing operate under nearly constant costs then *ceteris paribus* the optimal rate of growth of production and marketing will be determined by the optimal scale of R and D.

We begin by considering the determinants of the optimal scale of R and D.

Two of the major characteristics of R and D are the high degree of risk involved, and the importance of skilled labour inputs. R and D involves three main types of risk:

(1) The risk that the results obtained may be trivial or useless.

(2) The risk that because of the time-lags involved in R and D, the market environment may have changed radically by the time the research is completed.

(3) The risk that the final product may be copied or imitated.

The first type of risk is largely unavoidable; because research is carried out specifically to remedy ignorance, it is inevitable that the outcome of the research cannot be fully foreseen.

The time-lags involved in R and D are to some extent flexible: a project can be organised so that a large team spends a short time on it, or a small team a longer time. However, beyond a certain point there are diminishing returns to increasing the size of a team and reducing the time taken, due to the difficulties of co-ordinating individual efforts and speeding up individual pieces of work. It is, therefore, inevitable that for some R and D projects the optimal time-lag between initiation and completion will be relatively long.

The risk of imitation depends very much on the adequacy of patent protection. In the absence of protection, products embodying new marketing ideas can be imitated by competitors, and designs for producer durables embodying new technologies can be used by the manufacturer of the durable in supplying the firm's competitors. The first type of imitation can sometimes be discouraged by 'associative' advertising, whereby the firm convinces consumers that the qualities associated with the newly innovated product are to be identified with a particular brand name. The second type of imitation can only be resolved by backward integration into the manufacture of producer goods.

The risks associated with R and D are reflected directly in the scale of R and D and in the profitability of the firm, and indirectly in the rate of growth of the firm: a high degree of risk increases the firm's cost of capital, reduces investment in R and D, and hence the rate of growth, raises average profitability so that a high yield on risk capital is obtained, and increases the variability of profits from year to year.

The significance of skilled labour inputs for the optimal scale of R and D stems largely from an 'imperfection' in the market for skilled labour, namely the difficulty of organising long-term contracts in labour. This difficulty is essentially a legal and institutional one.

The skilled labour used for R and D normally requires on-the-job training. Individuals find it difficult to borrow to finance training, because of lenders' uncertainty; since the firm is particularly well placed to assess employees' prospects, the firm itself normally finances the training. In the absence of long-term contracts the firm therefore stands to lose considerably if the individual quits; alternatively, if the individual is made redundant the firm cannot recoup any of its investment by 'selling' the individual's outstanding contract to another firm.

Another aspect of the problem is that the knowledge produced by R and D is embodied in the minds of individual researchers. If these workers quit before the knowledge is fully documented then the investment is lost to the firm, while if they join competing firms, or set up rival businesses, even after the knowledge is documented, its commercial value to the firm is eliminated. Thus when exploiting knowledge the firm is potentially competing against some of its key employees.

The threat that employees will quit depends upon whether the knowledge and skills they possess are individual-specific or team-specific. If they are team-specific then no one individual knows enough to make it worth his while to leave, while the team as a whole cannot leave without destroying the equity market's trust in them. Thus team-specific assets are inseparable from the firm, and other firms cannot acquire them without buying the firm.

On the other hand, if knowledge and skills are individual-specific then workers can use the quit threat to appropriate the entire economic rent from the assets.

The principal constraints on the quit threat are obstacles to employee mobility. The obstacles may be natural ones, such as the costs of screening by alternative employers, or the costs of moving home (if applicable), or they may be deliberately imposed, such as the 'locking in' of employees by pension schemes, cheap mortgages, etc. To the extent that these obstacles reduce employee mobility, the expected cost of R and D is reduced, and hence the optimal scale of R and D is increased.

Two other influences on the optimal scale of R and D warrant special mention. The first is the coefficient of returns to scale in R and D, which depends very much on the type of research organisation appropriate to the industry. The second is the size of the potential market for the product, and the elasticities of consumer demand with respect to price and quality.

The analysis of the aggressive phase of the research-intensive firm is summarised in a simple mathematical model presented in the appendix to this chapter. It is shown that when knowledge is internalised and production and marketing operate under constant costs the optimal scale of R and D, and hence the rate of growth of the firm, depend on (i) the firm's cost of capital, which depends in turn on the market rate of interest and the degree of risk associated with R and D, (ii) the expected cost of skilled labour, which depends in turn on the market wage for skilled labour and the degree of inter-firm labour mobility, as reflected in the quit rate, (iii) the scale coefficient associated with the technology of R and D, and (iv) the parameters of demand for the firm's product. The profitability of the firm will be greater the greater are the risks associated with R and D (though the valuation of the firm will be less); otherwise profitability varies directly with the optimal scale of R and D and with the rate of growth of the firm.

The second stage in the life of the firm begins when the opportunities for further research along existing lines are exhausted.

If the skills of the research team are highly specific then their value will be eliminated. Research will cease, the rate of growth will fall and the profitability of the firm will diminish as imitators and substitutes erode its market power.

On the other hand, if the skills of the research team are fairly general then what happens will depend on whether the skills are individual- or team-specific. If they are individual-specific then the best policy will probably be to invite a takeover by a larger firm which can utilise the individuals more profitably within its own organisation. However, if the skills are team-specific then it may pay to redeploy the research team in some different, but related, area. The firm will continue to grow, but profitability will tend to be somewhat lower than before, and the activities of the firm will become more diversified.

2.5 The pattern of growth of MNEs explained by internalisation

The theory developed above can be used to explain the pattern of the growth of the MNEs in the twentieth century. We shall argue that prior to the Second World War multinationality was a by-product of the internalisation of intermediate-product markets in multistage production processes, and that post-war it is a by-product of the internalisation of markets in knowledge.

To establish the first proposition it must be shown that the types of multistage process with which multinationality was associated are those which meet the criteria of section 2.2. According to Vernon[7] and others the industries where multinationality predominated in the pre-war period were for primary products such as food, minerals and oil. According to section 2.2, the markets where internalisation is likely to be most advantageous are agricultural products, raw materials whose deposits are geographically concentrated, and intermediate products in capital-intensive manufacturing industries. The first two types of market embrace primary products such as food, minerals and oil. The only difficulty concerns why multinationality is not observed in capital-intensive manufacturing industries, such as steel. The analysis of location strategy in section 2.3 suggests a very simple answer: internalisation did indeed give rise to vertical integration in these industries, but the multiplant firms so created were localised, or at most multiregional. The relative lack of international specialisation at individual stages within these manufacturing industries is attributable to the fairly even spread of the relevant factor endowments. By contrast, the factors relevant to primary industries were very unevenly distributed, so that comparative advantage was important in promoting international specialisation at each stage.

To explain the post-war growth of MNEs in terms of the internalisation of knowledge it must be shown that in the post-war period the potential profitability of R and D activities has increased. The increase in profitability opportunities may be analysed in terms of shifts in demand and supply.

Derived demand for R and D has been stimulated by government needs for high technology goods – partly attributable to the arms and space races – by increasing consumer incomes which have stimulated demand for sophisticated consumer goods, and possibly also by social factors which have increased preferences for novelty and for continual improvements in product quality. In some cases these preferences may have been stimulated by innovating firms themselves, through advertising and through planned obsolescence.

On the supply side the costs of the major inputs to R and D have fallen significantly: skilled labour has become abundant

[7] R. Vernon, *Sovereignty at Bay* (London, 1971).

through the expansion of higher education, particularly in science and technology, while the invention of transistors, microcircuits, computers, etc. (themselves products of R and D) has significantly reduced the costs of R and D-oriented durable goods. These factors may also be attributable to government policies dictated by the arms and space races.

The typically large size of R and D-oriented MNEs may be attributed to an increase in the optimal scale of R and D in recent years. This is probably due to advances in organisation and methods. The traditional organisation of research – a few specialists working for many years on an isolated project – has been superseded by large interdisciplinary teams working for short periods on related groups of projects. The teamwork has been made possible by experience with wartime and post-war planning projects, and with arms and space race projects where the speeding up of innovation has been the top priority. Interdisciplinary co-operation has resulted from recognition of the similarity of research techniques in different fields of study, and the consequent breakdown of traditional academic divisions between subjects.

The post-war pattern of foreign direct investment – in particular cross-investment between developed economies – may also be explained in terms of the internalisation of knowledge. The investments of the R and D-intensive firm are oriented toward the search for knowledge of commercial potential and the exploitation of the firm's own proprietary knowledge. Government patronage of research, ease of communication with the more sophisticated consumers and easy access to skilled labour tend to favour firms based in developed economies. The costs of adapting knowledge to new markets and to new production environments tend to encourage these firms to invest in countries at a parallel stage of development, i.e. to invest in other developed economies rather than LDCs.

The growth and profitability of research-intensive MNEs may be explained in terms of the theory of section 2.4.

In the first stage of aggressive growth the more research-intensive is the firm the more likely it is to be multinational and the faster it is likely to grow; thus MNEs will tend to grow faster than average, not because of the advantages of multinationality *per se*, but because both multinationality and growth are linked to R and D through the internalisation of knowledge. A relationship between multinationality and profitability exists because of the relationship between multinationality and research-intensity on the one hand and between profitability and research-intensity on the other.

While the post-war growth of research-intensive MNEs is explained well by the strategy of aggressive expansion discussed above, very recent trends suggest that many MNEs may be entering on a second, more defensive, phase in their life. Depending on the nature of the firm's skills, this phase involves either the progressive decline of the firm, its takeover by another (usually larger) firm, or the redeployment of the research team on other projects. The first two possibilities raise awkward political issues in connection with the rationalisation of internationally owned firms, and the probability of widespread redundancies in their branch plants. On the other hand, the final possibility suggests that the growth of MNEs may continue, though at a reduced pace, and with their influence diversified over a wider range of industries. Policy discussions of MNEs have hitherto concentrated on the 'threats' posed by their continued growth, but it may be that in future more attention should be paid to the threat that, on the contrary, they may go into decline.

Appendix: A mathematical model of the growth of the research-intensive firm

The model is based on six key assumptions:

(1) The sole purpose of R and D is to develop improvements in product quality. Quality is measured somehow by index, Q, and the output of R and D by its rate of change, $\dot{Q}$.

(2) The average cost function of R and D is U-shaped; it is of the type associated with a Cobb–Douglas function with one or more fixed factors:

$$CRD = a + b\dot{Q}^{1/\beta} \qquad a,b > 0, \ \beta < 1 \qquad \text{(i)}$$

where CRD is the total cost of R and D; a and b are parameters which depend on the technological opportunities for R and D, the wage rate of skilled labour in the preferred location for R and D, and the quit rate; and β is a coefficient of returns to scale.

(3) Production and marketing operate under constant costs. Thus the total cost associated with servicing each market is proportional to the quantity sold:

$$CX_i = c_i X_i \qquad c_i > 0 \quad (i = 1, \ldots, n) \tag{ii}$$

where CX_i is the total cost of servicing the ith market, c_i is the unit cost, and X_i is the quantity sold.

(4) The firm can discriminate between regional markets, in each of which demand for its product depends on price, product quality, the prices and qualities of competing products, consumers' incomes, etc. Demand is of constant price-elasticity and is proportional to product quality; the prices and qualities of competing products and consumers' incomes are assumed to be exogenous:

$$X_i = d_i Q p_i^{-\gamma_i} \qquad d_i > 0, \quad \gamma_i > 1 \tag{iii}$$

where p_i is the price of the product and γ_i the price-elasticity of demand.

(5) All ideas for product improvements are implemented by the firm itself; no improvements are purchased or sold under licence.

(6) The objective of the management is to maximise the discounted sum of future profits;

$$\max \mathrm{NPV}_0 \int_0^\infty \exp(-rt) \Pi(t) dt \tag{iv}$$

where r is the firm's long-term cost of capital, which depends on the market rate of interest and the degree of risk associated with R and D, and Π is profit.

$$\Pi = (\sum_i (p_i X_i - CX_i) - CRD \tag{v}$$

Substituting (i)–(iii) into (v) and (v) into (iv), and then maximising with respect to p shows that just as in the static theory the optimal price in each market is equal to the marginal cost marked up by a percentage which depends solely on the elasticity of demand,

$$p_i = c_i \gamma_i / (\gamma_i - 1) \qquad (i = 1, \ldots, n) \tag{vi}$$

Since marginal cost is equal to average cost because of constant returns to scale, the absolute mark-up is independent of output, whence from the form of the demand function it follows that profit before deduction of R and D expenses is directly proportional to the quality of the product,

$$\sum_i (p_i X_i - CX_i) = eQ \tag{vii}$$

where

$$e = \sum_i d_i \gamma_i^{-\gamma_i} (c_i/(\gamma_i - 1))^{1-\gamma_i} \tag{viii}$$

Substituting (vii) into (iv) and solving the first-order conditions for a maximum with respect to $Q(t)$ shows that the optimal steady-state rate of product improvement is

$$\dot{Q} = (\beta e/(rb))^{\beta/(1-\beta)} \tag{ix}$$

Since price remains invariant, the scale of production increases at a rate proportional to the rate of product improvement,

$$\dot{X} = \sum \dot{X}_i = f \dot{Q} \tag{x}$$

where

$$f = \sum_i d_i (c_i \gamma_i/(\gamma_i - 1))^{-\gamma_i} \tag{xi}$$

Since the scale of R and D and hence the rate of product improvement are constant over time it follows from equations (i), (v) and (vii) that profits increase over time at a constant rate which is proportional to the scale of R and D,

$$\dot{\Pi} = e\dot{Q} \tag{xii}$$

Substituting (xii) into (iv) and evaluating the integral gives the value of the firm as

$$NPV_0 = (eQ_0 - a + [(e/r) - b]\dot{Q})/r \tag{xiii}$$

where NPV_0 is the net present value of the profit stream at time zero, and Q_0 is the initial quality of the product.

Equations (ix) and (x) indicate that the scale of R and D, and hence the rate of growth of the firm, will be greater the greater are the returns to scale in R and D (measured by β), the greater is the profitability of production (measured by e), the lower is the cost of capital (measured by r) and the lower are the variable costs (measured by b). Equation (xiii) shows that the value of the firm also varies directly with the scale of R and D, and in addition varies directly with the initial quality of the product (measured by Q_0) and inversely with the fixed costs of R and D (measured by a). An inverse relationship between the value of the firm and the cost of capital (reflecting in part the risks of R and D) is also apparent.

The case where the impact of R and D is on technology rather than on product quality may be analysed in a similar way, though the results are more complex because of the dependency of pricing policy on the changing cost structure.

3 Alternative Theories of the Multinational Enterprise

3.1 Introduction

This chapter compares and contrasts the theory expounded in Chapter 2 with alternative theories of the MNE. Our review is confined to theories which focus on the impact of the market environment on the multinationalism of individual firms. Questions concerning the aggregate impact of multinationalism on trade and investment flows are not considered.

Our thesis is that, with one or two exceptions, the alternative theories can be synthesised within the general theory presented in the previous chapter. Furthermore the synthesis highlights certain methodological short-comings common to many of the theories. In particular, as originally formulated;

(1) They prejudge some of the crucial issues, such as the decision to internalise a market.

(2) They are often vague about the assumptions on which their analysis is based, in particular the objectives of firms and the competitive constraints to which they are subject.

(3) They fail to distinguish between short-run and long-run analysis (e.g. the long-run growth of the firm is analysed by taking endowments of proprietary knowledge, etc. to be fixed, which is only true in the short-run, because in the long run they are determined by the firm's investment policy).

3.2 The Hymer–Kindleberger (HK) theory[1]

The HK theory is addressed to the question of why a foreign-owned firm is able to compete with indigenous firms in the host economy, given the innate advantages of an indigenous firm. Firstly, the indigenous firm has a knowledge of consumer tastes, the legal and institutional framework of business, and local business customs which the foreign firm can only acquire at a cost. Secondly, the foreign firm incurs costs of operating at a distance, costs not only of travel, communication and time lost in communicating information and decisions, but also costs of misunderstandings that lead to errors. According to the HK theory the foreign-owned firm must possess some compensating advantages which allow it to compete on equal terms with indigenous firms.

These advantages may be general advantages shared by all firms of certain nationalities, as suggested by Aliber (see section 3.3). However, most writers in the HK tradition have focused on advantages which are specific to individual firms. In order for these firm-specific advantages to be exploitable in foreign countries they must be readily transferable within the firm. Kindleberger[2] lists a number of potential advantages, which include ownership of a brand name, the possession of special marketing skills, access to patented or generally unavailable technology, favoured access to sources of finance, team-specific managerial skills, plant economies of scale, and economies of vertical integration. The list is comprehensive, but gives little clue as to which of the advantages is most important in practice.

Johnson[3] has suggested that the more significant advantages have the characteristic of a 'public good' within the firm, i.e. they can be exploited by a subsidiary of the parent firm without any additional cost to the parent or to the subsidiaries already exploiting it. The prototypical firm-specific public good is special knowledge or skill. Caves (see section 3.4) has argued

---

[1] The seminal work is S. Hymer, 'The International Operations of International Firms: A Study of Direct Investment', unpublished Ph.D. dissertation, Massachusetts Institute of Technology, 1960.

[2] C. P. Kindleberger, *American Business Abroad* (New Haven, 1969), p. 14.

[3] H. G. Johnson, 'The Efficiency and Welfare Implications of the International Corporation', in *The International Corporation*, ed. C. P. Kindleberger (Cambridge, Mass., 1970).

that the most important skill is the ability to differentiate a product, while Hirsch[4] emphasises the advantage conferred by knowledge obtained from past R and D.

While the possession of an internationally transferable advantage is a necessary condition for the foreign firm to be competitive, it does not guarantee that the firm itself finds it profitable to produce abroad. Given the costs of 'foreignness' it is quite possible that the firm will prefer either to licence its advantage, or to produce at home and service foreign markets by exports. Thus to produce abroad the firm must not only have an advantage, but the economic rent accruing from that advantage must be enhanced by foreign production.

Why should production abroad be more profitable than licensing the advantage to a foreign producer? Hymer argues that it is because of imperfections in the markets for patents and other forms of knowledge. Why should production abroad be preferred to production at home? The answer depends upon whether production abroad involves local production or third-country production. The main reason for choosing third-country production is to exploit international factor-price differentials. An obvious reason for local production is the avoidance of transport and tariff costs. However, it has been argued by Caves that local production is preferred mainly because a local producer is better placed to undertake modifications to the product to adapt it to local conditions and tastes. This view is related to the theory of product differentiation, and is examined in more detail in section 3.4.

The essence of the HK theory is that there are two barriers to market servicing: barriers to trade which prevent the MNE from maximising returns by exporting, and barriers which prevent indigenous firms from producing a competitive product – specifically, the inability of indigenous firms to acquire the necessary proprietary knowledge. There are thus fairly obvious similarities between the HK theory and the theory expounded in Chapter 2. However, there are also important differences.

Firstly, in the HK theory the advantages of the firm – in particular its endowments of proprietary knowledge – are taken

---

[4] S. Hirsch, 'An International Trade and Investment Theory of the Firm', *Discussion Papers in International Investment and Business Studies*, University of Reading, 17 (1974), forthcoming in *Economica*.

as given. Because there is no explanation of how the advantages are generated, they appear in the theory as windfall gains, or 'manna from Heaven'. The planning and investment necessary to build up the advantages are ignored. This means that the theory overstates the average profitability of firms exploiting these advantages, because it ignores altogether their costs of acquisition.

Secondly, because costs of acquisition are ignored it is impossible for the HK theory to explain or predict why firms invest in these advantages rather than in other types of asset. The net present-value criterion of investment appraisal indicates that the discounted future returns from investment in the advantage must exceed the present and future costs incurred. Without a theory of how the costs of acquiring advantages vary with the scale of the investment in R and D it is impossible to explain the optimal level of investment in firm-specific advantages. This means for example that without further elaboration the HK theory is unable to explain the growth of firm-specific advantages in the post-war period.

In contrast, our theory provides a much more accurate and precise account of the origin of the attribute, or set of attributes, that give the MNE its advantages. We regard such advantages as the rewards for past investment in (i) R and D facilities which create an advantage in technological fields, (ii) the creation of an integrated team of skills, the rent from which is greater than the sum of the rewards to individuals, and therefore accruing to 'the firm' and within which individuals, as such, are dispensable, (iii) the creation of an information transmission network which allows the benefits of (i) and (ii) to be transmitted at low cost within the organisation, but also protects such information, including knowledge of market conditions, from outsiders.

Thirdly, the HK theory predisposes one to think in terms of a single innovation or patent. If this were the case, then perhaps licensing would be a more appropriate form of exploitation. Even though the full rent might not be appropriated, the firm does not have to incur the additional costs of overseas production. Our theory lays emphasis on the transmission of the *ability to* innovate. An investment policy such as we outline leads to a stream of innovations which in the ascendency phase of the MNE and its industry produce the dynamic for growth.

3.3   Aliber's theory of the MNE as a currency-area phenomenon[5]

Aliber's theory of the MNE falls within the Hymer–Kindleberger tradition, in the sense that it is oriented toward a search for an advantage of the foreign-owned firm over its domestic competitors. But Aliber argues that this advantage is not specific to individual firms, but to all firms based in a particular currency area. To explain Aliber's theory we must first elucidate the concept of a currency premium.

In the international financial capital market a debt may be denominated in any one of several currencies. The holder of such debt bears a risk that the currency in which it is denominated may depreciate relative to other currencies. If investors as a whole have no aversion to risk then the rate of interest on a debt denominated in any given currency will exactly reflect the expected rate of depreciation of the currency. But if investors as a whole are averse to risk, the rate of interest on debt will carry a premium which reflects the uncertainty of the market with respect to the rate of depreciation: it is said that the debt bears a currency premium to compensate the investor for exchange risk.

Aliber's argument is based on the assertion that portfolio investors are myopic: they assume that the foreign investments of MNEs are all in the same currency area as the parent firm. Because investments in other currency areas are overlooked, the investors take no account of the exchange risks involved in the repatriation of profits to the parent firm. Thus the assets of a US firm operating in the UK are valued by the market as though they were dollar assets instead of sterling assets. It follows that if the currency premium on dollars is lower than the currency premium on sterling (dollars are the preferred currency) then the market rate of interest on the debt of the US-based MNE will be lower than on the debt of an indigenous UK firm, after allowance for expected currency depreciation. Thus the US-based MNE can borrow more cheaply than the UK firm to finance any form of capital expenditure in the UK. One implication of this is that a US firm can realise an immediate profit by financing the takeover of a UK firm.

[5] See R. Z. Aliber, 'A Theory of Direct Investment', in *The International Corporation*, ed. C. P. Kindleberger (Cambridge, Mass., 1970), pp. 17–34; and 'The Multinational Enterprise in a Multiple Currency World', *The Multinational Enterprise*, ed. J. H. Dunning (London, 1971), pp. 49–56.

Aliber's argument can be extended to the case where the asset acquired is in some third country; so long as the dollar is the preferred currency the US firm can profit by buying out the interest of a UK firm in a third country. In fact there is nothing to stop the US firm from raising the money in London to finance the takeover of the UK firm, so long as investors in the London stock market believe that they are acquiring a 100 per cent dollar asset.

The strength of Aliber's theory is that it predicts well the direction of the post-war expansion of MNEs – in particular the American takeover of Europe in the fifties and sixties, and the Japanese takeover of south-east Asia in the late sixties and early seventies. The recent decline in the strength of the dollar and the improvement in the mark may also explain the downturn in American overseas expansion and the resurgence of German multinationalism.

However there are reasons to doubt whether the type of myopia postulated by Aliber is still prevalent in the capital markets of the seventies. It may have been true of the transitional phase when MNEs first entered capital markets on a large scale, but it is difficult to believe that it persists today in the minds of institutional investment managers – if Aliber's theory is correct then well-informed investors will presumably have modified their behaviour in the light of it. It is possible that investment managers rely on non-institutional investors to maintain the myopic valuation, but the predominance of institutional investment in the market argues against this.

While Aliber's theory explains both the existence and the direction of foreign direct investment between currency areas, it is unable to explain anything about capital flows within currency areas: the investment of US firms within the dollar area, for example. Neither can it account for cross-investment between currency areas – the fact that US firms invest in Europe at the same time as European firms invest in the US. Nor does it explain why firms incur substantial costs in setting up factories abroad when they can profit from investor myopia simply by taking over going concerns. Indeed, Aliber fails to explain why holding companies have not been set up with the express purpose of capitalising on investor myopia; it may be that some firms have done just this under the cover of legitimate productive operations, but it is certain that there are many MNEs that have not.

3.4 Diversification and the MNE

It is often suggested that foreign direct investment is the result of a conscious effort by management to diversify the firm's activities. In section 1.5 we distinguished three main types of diversification: horizontal, vertical and conglomerate. Each of these may be regarded as an alternative strategy for exploiting the advantages of diversification. On this view the post-war growth of horizontal and conglomerate diversification, and perhaps also the pre-war growth of vertical integration, are different aspects of the same general phenomenon.

Authors differ about the nature of the advantages of diversification. The role of diversification in spreading risks is considered separately in section 3.9, so that the issues it raises can be discussed at greater length.

Caves[6] regards diversification as a means of exploiting a general ability of the firm to differentiate a product, i.e. to design a product which has a mix of attributes with a wide appeal to consumers. Suppose that preferences for product attributes are similar over a wide range of products, but vary marginally within individual regions or nations and within product groups. The ability to differentiate a product can be exploited either by differentiating the same product across different regions, or by differentiating a wide range of products to the tastes of one region, or by some mixture of the two. The first strategy leads to horizontal diversification and the second to conglomerate diversification. If there are advantages in specialising in one particular type of diversification then we shall observe two distinct types of firm: the MNE specialised in a single product or narrow group of products, and the uni-national conglomerate specialised in a single country, but marketing a broad range of products. It is Caves's insight that these two apparently separate phenomena may in reality be interdependent.

A more general view of the advantages of diversification is

[6] R. E. Caves, 'International Corporations: the Industrial Economics of Foreign Investment', *Economica*, 38 (1971), 1–27.

provided by the theory of excess managerial capacity.[7] The activities of the firm may require the deployment of certain indivisible factors, which cannot be fully utilised without some expansion in the scale of the firm's operations. The prototypical indivisible factors are the services of highly specialised managerial personnel. If the scale of the firm's existing operations is limited by the size of the market, or by the reactions of oligopolistic competitors, then its scale can be expanded only by venturing into new markets. Once this expansion has occurred, however, it may be optimal to employ other types of indivisible factor, and this will generate a further incentive to expand by diversification. Eventually, the various indivisible factors will become combined in proportions which allow each to be fully utilised, and the growth of the firm will level off.

Both of the above theories are based on the internalisation of knowledge, in the first case knowledge of how to differentiate a product, and in the second case knowledge of how to carry out certain specialised managerial functions. The excess managerial capacity theory adds a new dimension to the analysis, however, by introducing indivisible factors in management, which increase the optimal size of the management team, and thereby increase the optimal scale of the firm's activities as a whole.

3.5 Vernon's product-cycle (PC) theory, Mark I[8]

The PC theory distinguishes three main phases in the life cycle of a product. Analysis of the first phase is concerned mainly with what determines the initial location of production. Analysis of the second phase focuses on whether emerging foreign markets are serviced by export or by foreign investment, while in the third phase the theory concentrates on the competitiveness of foreign production *vis-à-vis* local firms.

The key assumptions of the PC theory are that:

(1) Tastes differ according to income.

[7] This theory is implicit in several recent works on the MNE. For an early development of these ideas see E. A. G. Robinson, 'The Problem of Management and the Size of Firms', *Economic Journal*, 44 (1934), 242–57.

[8] R. Vernon, 'International Investment and International Trade in the Product Cycle', *Quarterly Journal of Economics*, 80 (1966), 190–207.

   (2) Communication costs within the firm, and between the firm and the market, are significant and increase with distance.

   (3) Products undergo predictable changes in technology and marketing methods.

   (4) The market in technical know-how is very imperfect.

The final assumption is not made explicit by Vernon, but is necessary in order to sustain his argument.

The first phase of the cycle is the innovative *new-product* stage, where new wants express themselves, or cost conditions favour some new method of production. Vernon argues that the major force generating new wants has been increasing *per capita* incomes, and the main incentive to technical innovation has been labour scarcity, which has encouraged the development of labour-saving producer goods. The changes are felt initially in some particular regional or national market – the most 'advanced' market – and occur elsewhere only as income levels and labour scarcity in other markets catch up. In the twentieth century the most advanced market has been the US.

Because of communication costs entrepreneurs are more conscious of opportunities the closer they are to the market. It follows that product innovation is first undertaken by businessmen whose activities are located in the advanced market. Initially the product is unstandardised because of the need for continual adaptation and improvement of the design to suit customers' needs, and for improvement of product technology through experimentation with alternative inputs. Because communication between production and marketing needs to be frequent, and communication costs increase with distance, it is important to locate production close to the market.

The second phase is that of the *maturing product*. As a result of 'learning by doing' the less efficient product designs and production methods are weeded out, the need for flexibility declines, and the form of the product is stabilised. Buyer knowledge increases, demand becomes more price-elastic, and the firm becomes increasingly sensitive to routine production costs. Because technology has stabilised it is not so important for production to be close to the market. The market expands as

income increases and opportunities appear for exploiting economies of scale. When foreign markets first appear they are serviced by exports, and the exporting phase continues so long as
the sum of the marginal production costs in the home country
and marginal transport costs is less than the average cost of
production overseas. Depending on labour cost differentials
between home and overseas, it eventually becomes economic
to invest abroad. Typically, investment occurs first in high-
income countries where demand patterns follow those of the
innovating country, and where labour costs are relatively low.
Thus for example US firms tend to invest first in Western Europe.

The final stage is that of the *standardised product*, where the
product is completely uniform and undifferentiable, and competition between producers is based solely on price. Market
information is no longer a problem and the need is now for the
lowest-cost source of supply. The most labour-intensive stages
of production are thus transferred to developing countries.

There are many similarities between the PC theory and the
theory presented in Chapter 2: in particular the emphasis on
technological innovation and product improvement, and the
impact of these factors on the location strategy of the firm. A
virtue of the PC theory is the constant attention paid to the
interaction of supply and demand factors, and to the channels
of communication between the market and the firm. This gives
a more convincing and coherent view of the sources of US firms'
advantages than do the other theories examined in this chapter.

The PC theory successfully relates the exports of US industries to the degree of product innovation and non-standardisa-
tion.[9] It suggests that the post-war acceleration of US foreign
investment is a response to either a reducing lag between innovation and standardisation, or to increasing consumer preferences
for new standardised products. The first explanation is endorsed
by Servan-Schreiber,[10] and the second by Galbraith.[11] There is

[9] See G. C. Hufbauer, 'The Impact of National Characteristics and Technology
on the Commodity Composition of Trade in Manufactured Goods', in *The
Technology Factor in International Trade*, ed. R. Vernon (New York, 1970),
145–213; and L. T. Wells, *The Product Life Cycle and International Trade*
(Cambridge, Mass., 1972).

[10] J. J. Servan-Schreiber, *The American Challenge* (translated by R. Steel)
(London, 1968).

[11] J. K. Galbraith, *The New Industrial State* (London, 1967).

a great deal to be said for both explanations, though as yet no conclusive evidence is available.

However, the PC theory cannot account for the increasing proportion of foreign investment which is not export-substituting, e.g. US investment in European food-processing industries. This comparatively recent phenomenon might conceivably be interpreted as a limiting case of the product cycle in which the standardisation-lag tends to zero. However, this does not explain other characteristics of recent foreign investment, e.g. the tendency for non-standardised products to be produced abroad, and for products to be carefully differentiated to suit the local market.

It appears that while the product cycle is an accurate description of the pre-war and early post-war growth of MNEs, recent trends have outdated it; in particular the process of product development and innovation has become highly organised, so that products are no longer planned for one market and then transferred to another, but planned and differentiated at the outset to suit different tastes in different markets; the firm with international horizons no longer considers product innovation as a 'one-off' job, but as a continuous process. The R and D theory captures this pattern of behaviour much better than does the PC theory.

There are also two methodological objections to the PC theory.

Firstly, although the PC theory is apparently dynamic, in the sense that it concerns evolution through time, it is in fact only programmatic: it predicts the sequence in which events occur, but not the rate at which they occur, or the time-lags which separate them. It is therefore easily fitted to data by suitably adjusting the time-periods associated with each phase of the cycle. Correspondingly, although it can be used to predict what will happen next, it does not tell us how soon the predicted event will occur. In contrast, the theory presented in Chapter 2 explains the growth and location policies of the firm as functions of key exogenous variables, and given the values of these variables and their rates of change, it predicts precisely at what rate and in what direction the firm will evolve.

Secondly, the PC theory considers each of the three decisions – how much to invest in product development, how to service a foreign market, and how to compete with overseas firms – as quite separate decisions made at different stages of the cycle. But a rational decision-taker cannot isolate the three decisions in this way as the theory of Chapter 2 indicates: the decisions are all interdependent, so that a rational decision-taker must consider them all simultaneously. The programmatic decision process of the PC theory is thus a considerable oversimplification of problems facing the international firm.

3.6 Vernon's product-cycle theory, Mark II[12]

Later writings by Vernon have substantially modified the PC theory. The emphasis has been shifted to oligopolistic behaviour, and the desire of firms to maintain an oligopolistic market structure by erecting barriers to entry.

The first stage of the cycle, *innovation-based oligopoly*, is much the same as before, except that on the supply side not only are labour-saving innovations recognised, but also land-saving (Western European) and material-saving (Japanese) ones.

The second stage of the cycle, *mature oligopoly*, is very different. Economies of scale in production, marketing and research constitute an effective entry barrier, behind which rival firms, each sensitive to the other's actions, play out a business game. Each player nullifies aggressive strategies initiated by the others, by matching them move for move. A leader entering a virgin market is immediately followed by his rivals. The ultimate sanction against a rival is the instigation of a price war: because tariffs tend to immunise firms from price competition through imports, firms set up production in their rivals' major markets to strengthen their bargaining position. The ultimate aim is to stabilise the world-market shares of the rival firms, stability being achieved when each of the rival firms produces in each of the world's major markets.[13]

The final stage is *senescent oligopoly*, in which economies of scale cease to be an effective deterrent to entry, and after attempting to erect other barriers, e.g. by differentiating their product

[12] R. Vernon, *Sovereignty at Bay* (London, 1971); and 'The Location of Economic Activity', in *Economic Analysis and the Multinational Enterprise*, ed. J. H. Dunning (London, 1974), pp. 89–114.

[13] Similar views are expressed in R. Rowthorn, *International Big Business, 1957–67* (Cambridge, 1972).

through advertising, the producers reconcile themselves to competitive pressures. Some leave the industry altogether while others, who may have favoured access to factor supplies, stay on. In this way the location of production at last becomes determined by competitive forces acting on interregional cost differentials.

Empirical support for the PC Mark II theory is presented in a painstaking work by Knickerbocker of the post-war US penetration of overseas markets which is reviewed in the following section.

3.7 Foreign investment as oligopolistic reaction

According to Knickerbocker[14] the timing of foreign investment is determined largely by reaction to competitors' investments; he argues that the optimal strategy for firms in an oligopolistic industry is to match their rivals move for move. Once one firm invests in a particular region, the optimal strategy for the other firms is to 'follow the leader', even if this confers no immediate advantage on the follower, but simply spoils the market for the leader. Knickerbocker's theory implies that the initial investments of foreign enterprises in a given market will tend to be 'bunched' in time, and that this bunching will tend to be greater the more oligopolistic the industry. Knickerbocker tests his theory on the data for 187 large US-based MNEs, described in Chapter 1. He shows that bunching is positively correlated across industries with the four-firm concentration ratio, which is used as an index of oligopolistic performance. He shows also that bunching is strongly correlated with profitability, and with an index of the stability and cohesion of the national market.

While Knickerbocker's results support his hypothesis they also support a rival hypothesis which has nothing to do with oligopolistic behaviour. The hypothesis is simply that firms maximise profit in a world where information about market conditions is unequally distributed. To illustrate, suppose that there is an exogenous change in market conditions, such as a fall in factor prices in a certain region. The firm with the best market-intelligence system will be the first to recognise the opportunity for investment and sooner or later will decide to

[14] F. T. Knickerbocker, *Oligopolistic Reaction and the Multinational Enterprise* (Cambridge, Mass., 1973).

exploit it, e.g. by relocating production in the region. Because knowledge is unequally distributed between firms, the actions of firms with superior market-intelligence systems will be monitored by other firms. Thus the action of the firm in undertaking the investment will draw the attention of other firms to changes in market conditions which have created similar investment opportunities for them. On re-examining their market strategies, they may decide to follow suit – not as part of an oligopolistic strategy, but simply in response to market information acquired through monitoring the moves of other firms. Thus the fact that a large number of firms invest in the same region at about the same time may indicate no more than that they are all responsive to the same set of market conditions.

The speed with which firms respond to a move by the initiating firm will depend on the extent to which they arrive at a similar, or more favourable, view of the investment opportunities. If there is a high degree of uncertainty or the initiating firm does not appear to be doing very well then firms may defer their investment so that they can benefit from the experience of the initiator. On the other hand, if there is little uncertainty or the initiating firm is earning high profits, firms will tend to respond very quickly. The theory therefore predicts that, across industries, bunching of foreign investment will be positively associated with profitability and with the stability and cohesion of the market concerned. This agrees well with Knickerbocker's results, although it does not directly imply an association between bunching and concentration. However, once it is recognised that profitability and concentration are highly correlated across industries, for different but well-known reasons, it is evident that a significant correlation between bunching and profitability will tend to produce a significant correlation between bunching and concentration. Only an examination of the first-order partial correlation between bunching and concentration, with profitability held constant, would confirm or refute Knickerbocker's hypothesis.

Until this investigation has been carried out we would argue that our own hypothesis is to be preferred, because Knickerbocker's hypothesis is not only more complicated, but its logical foundations are more open to criticism. To begin with, in Knickerbocker's theory the objectives of the firm are never clearly stated; are they profit-maximisation, managerial risk-aversion, growth-maximisation, maintenance of market share, or a desire for multinationality *per se*? Secondly, it is never clearly shown, with reference to one or more of these objectives, why a certain strategy is optimal. The only firm conclusion of oligopoly theory is that the less predictable a firm's behaviour is to others, the less able are other firms to take advantage of it. It follows that in most circumstances a 'randomised strategy'[15] is preferable to a systematic mode of behaviour. This suggests that if it is a regular code of behaviour for firms to 'follow the leader' irrespective of the profitability of the leader's strategy, then the leader should be able to turn this predictable pattern of behaviour to his own advantage. It is therefore difficult to see why a predictable strategy of following the leader should be optimal under oligopoly, whatever the objectives of management happen to be. Finally it should be emphasised that Knickerbocker's theory, in contrast to the rival theory outlined in Chapter 2, offers no explanation of the investment behaviour of the initiating firm.

3.8 Foreign investment as a behavioural process

According to Aharoni[16] the timing of foreign investment depends very much on chance stimuli, and on the way management processes convert these stimuli into decisions to invest. The propensity of the firm to invest depends on the strength and frequency of these stimuli to investment, which may come from within the firm, e.g. a self-interested proposal originating from a manager, or from without, e.g. a tariff increase by a foreign government which alters the balance between export and investment. Once an investment project has been formulated a search is initiated for information relevant to its appraisal. During the search some members of the search team acquire a commitment to the project because of the time and effort they have expended on it. If their appraisal of the project succeeds in correcting the natural pessimism of top management then it leads to a decision to invest.

[15] See J. Von Neumann and O. Morgenstern, *Theory of Games and Economic Behaviour*, 2nd ed. (Princeton, 1947), ch. 14, p. 17.

[16] Y. Aharoni, *The Foreign Investment Decision Process* (Cambridge, Mass., 1966).

Aharoni believes that the evidence from his case studies conflicts with the profit-maximisation hypothesis, although in fact it is broadly consistent with profit-maximisation under uncertainty, as Stevens indicates.[17] Aharoni's refutation of profit-maximisation appears to be based on a confusion of ends and means;[18] the behaviour he describes is basically an organised search procedure, albeit an inefficient one. The principal inefficiencies are the lack of routine scanning of the business environment for new projects, and the overcommitment of certain managers to the projects they are appraising. However, the firms interviewed by Aharoni were generally new to the international scene, and it is reasonable to suppose that these inefficiencies will be reduced once the firms become accustomed to international operations.

3.9 Diversification and the spreading of risk through foreign investment

Some recent empirical studies of foreign direct investment assume that the MNE is in a situation analogous to that of an individual investor choosing a portfolio of risky assets.[19] The individual usually invests in financial assets such as government debt, equities, and industrial debentures whereas the firm tends to invest in real assets, such as different types of plant and equipment, or plants in different locations. The principles underlying the choice of asset are alleged to be the same in both cases.

The theory of portfolio choice postulates that the investor is risk-averse, that is, he is prepared to pay less than its expected value for the outcome of a risky project. The rational investor chooses a portfolio which, for a given expected return, minimises the risk of the portfolio, as measured, say, by the variance of the return; such a portfolio is said to be efficient. It has been shown by Markowitz[20] that when assets are traded in competitive markets an efficient portfolio is normally diversified over

[17] G. V. G. Stevens, 'The Determinants of Investment', in *Economic Analysis and the Multinational Enterprise*, ed. J. H. Dunning (London, 1974), pp. 47–88.

[18] J. H. Dunning, 'The Determinants of International Production', *Oxford Economic Papers*, 25 (1973), 289–336.

[19] G. V. G. Stevens, 'Capital Mobility and the International Firm' and M. F. J. Prachowny, 'Direct Investment and the Balance of Payments of the United States', both in *International Mobility and Movement of Capital*, eds. F. Machlup, W. S. Salant and L. Tarshis (New York, 1972).

[20] H. M. Markowitz, *Portfolio Analysis* (New Haven, 1970).

most of the available assets, and the assets which predominate in the portfolio are ones for which the ratio of the expected return to the variance of the return is high and between which the correlations of the returns are low, or negative. The theory of portfolio choice has been used with limited success to explain diversification of individual shareholdings by industry or by country, and diversification of liquid-asset holdings between cash and various forms of short-term debt.[21] However, we shall argue that the theory which applies to an individual investor cannot be applied to a corporate direct investor such as an MNE.

Firstly, because an MNE is a corporation it is quite unnecessary for it to diversify for its shareholders' benefit since the shareholders can diversify as much as they wish by spreading their shareholdings over different MNEs. Thus the advantages of diversification at the individual level do not extend to the corporate level. Only in so far as there are obstacles to individual diversification is corporate diversification desirable from the shareholders' point of view.

The second objection concerns the role of the firm as a direct investor. The essence of direct investment is that it involves not just ownership of a share in an asset but the acquisition of a controlling interest in it; in most cases a controlling interest involves holding a fairly substantial proportion (if not a majority) of the equity. However, it can be shown that the holding of a controlling interest in any assets but very small ones will normally represent a suboptimal degree of diversification, because it involves a fairly substantial proportion of the portfolio being tied up in a single holding. There is thus a *prima facie* case that a portfolio designed to reduce risk through diversification will not consist of direct investments, but of relatively small shareholdings in a large number of assets.

The case for analysing corporate direct investment in terms of portfolio choice rests on the existence of imperfections in the equity market which (i) impede diversification by individuals and favour diversification through intermediaries such as firms and investment trusts, and (ii) reduce the optimal diversification of intermediaries so that diversification through controlling

---

[21] For further details see H. G. Grubel, 'Internationally Diversified Portfolios', *American Economic Review*, 58 (1968), 1299–1314.

interests (such as the direct investments of a multiplant firm) is efficient relative to diversification through a larger number of smaller shareholdings (such as the portfolio of an investment trust).

Transaction costs in the equity market are sufficient to produce both effects, provided they are large enough. If transaction costs are defined narrowly in terms of brokerage charges, etc., then although they may be significant enough to persuade the small investor to resort to intermediaries, they are unlikely to tip the balance in favour of diversification through direct investment. However if transaction costs are broadly defined to include the costs of acquiring information about the prospective returns on an investment then, where business activities are highly complex and the cost to outsiders of acquiring information is high, there may be a strong incentive for some intermediaries to restrict their portfolio to large holdings of just a few assets. Under conditions of unequal distribution of knowledge in the equity market a pyramid structure of diversification may evolve. At the top of the pyramid is the individual who holds shares in a limited number of investment trusts which are well known to him; at the next level each investment trust holds an influential interest in a limited number of large firms, and at the final level each firm holds a controlling interest in a number of subsidiaries.

It can be argued that the increasing complexity of modern business – not unconnected with the rapid post-war increase in R and D – has created a strong incentive to the evolution of the pyramid structure; this incentive is reflected in a premium on the equity valuation of diversified firms. However, it should be emphasised that the pattern of diversification is such that the firm will diversify into activities about which, relative to the market, it has the greatest knowledge, and that such a strategy of diversification is quite different from that suggested by previous studies of foreign direct investment based on the portfolio approach.

Some writers would justify the application of the portfolio-choice model in terms of the divorce of ownership and control.[22] In an imperfect capital market, managers can pursue policies

[22] For a recent survey see J. R. Wildsmith, *Managerial Theories of the Firm* (London, 1973).

which conflict with shareholders' preferences, within the constraint that the value of the firm is not reduced by more than the cost of a takeover. It is often argued that the objectives of managers differ from those of shareholders because, unlike shareholders, managers are rewarded only partly by dividends, and mainly by salaries which are only indirectly related to the profitability of the firm. Managers may therefore be more risk-averse than shareholders and put the safeguarding of salaries and jobs before earning a profit. If managers overvalue risk and undervalue profit relative to the market then, it is argued, managers may diversify the firm's activities to suit their own ends. Diversification through direct investment is preferable to managers because it widens the scope of their discretion. However as an explanation of foreign direct investment the theory does not work well. It must be recognised that there are other risk-reducing strategies besides diversification: increasing holdings of liquid assets, for example, and the avoidance of high-risk activities such as R and D. Only if foreign direct investment was associated with high liquidity and low levels of R and D could it be inferred that it was the product of the overvaluation of risk by certain firms. This hypothesis is convincingly refuted by the empirical evidence presented in the next chapter.

4 The World's Largest Firms

4.1 Introduction
This chapter presents econometric evidence on the theory developed in Chapter 2. Section 4.2 describes the sample, which is based on a world-wide cross-section of large manufacturing firms, and indicates how the key variables have been measured. Section 4.3 develops and summarises the predictions of the theory, emphasising how the hypotheses can be formulated so as to be testable within the limits imposed by data availability. Section 4.4 reviews the statistical methodology. Section 4.5 presents formal tests of the hypotheses. Section 4.6 discusses possible mis-specifications of the statistical relationships and describes tests which have been made to check the sensitivity of the results to specification error. Section 4.7 summarises the main conclusions of the study.

4.2 The sample data[1]
The sample covers manufacturing firms reported in the *Fortune* lists of the 500 largest US firms and 300 largest non-US firms. The restriction to manufacturing firms excludes utilities such as AT and T and retailing firms such as Sears Roebuck. Some of the firms are majority-owned subsidiaries (e.g. Western Electric) while others (e.g. BP) are wholly or partly nationalised. The firms included in the sample all appeared continuously in the *Fortune* lists between 1967 and 1972, and avoided any major reorganisation during this period; this criterion reduced the number of eligible non-US firms to 170. It was decided to limit

[1] For a full description of the data see J. H. Dunning and R. D. Pearce *Profitability and Performance of the World's Largest Industrial Companie* (London, 1975).

the coverage of US firms to those whose size was comparable with the non-US firms; the sample therefore includes just 264 US firms with sales of over $300 million in 1972, giving a total of 434 firms in the sample.

To test in detail the main propositions of the theory the following data are required on each firm: R and D expenditure, growth rate, profitability, size, capital-intensity, nationality of the parent firm and the international and interregional distribution of the firm's operations, as measured, for example, by the proportion of value added effected in each host country. There are two major short-comings of the data: information on R and D expenditure is available only by industry and not by firm, and secondly, an international and interregional breakdown of operations by host country is available only for a very limited number of firms – for most of the firms only a summary measure of the degree of multinationality is available. This lack of information on the subsidiaries of the MNE means that it is not possible to analyse the role of 'region-specific factors' (see section 2.1).

A surrogate measure of R and D-intensity is obtained for each firm by classifying firms by industry group and then classifying the industry groups by R and D-intensity. Fifteen basic industry groups were distinguished, and as Table 4.1

TABLE 4.1 Frequency distribution of firms by industry.

	Number of firms
Oil	41
Motor vehicles	19
Rubber	6
Tobacco	6
Paper	15
Chemicals and pharmaceuticals	41
Aircraft	8
Iron and steel	24
Food and drink	38
Packaging	7
Textiles and apparel	15
Electrical engineering	45
Non-electrical engineering	56
Non-ferrous metals	17
Stone, clay, glass and miscellaneous	29
Conglomerates based on food, chemicals, etc.	41
Conglomerates based on engineering, metals, etc.	26
Total	434

shows, about 82 per cent of the firms may be classified to just one of those industries on the basis of published listings of their products. The remaining 67 firms are conglomerates of one kind or another; 41 of these firms are based largely on food, chemicals, etc. (type I conglomerates) and 26 on engineering and metals (type II conglomerates). The 17 industrial categories (including the two conglomerate categories) are classified by R and D-intensity as follows. According to section 2.3, two main types of R and D may be distinguished, depending on whether the innovations effected are technical or marketing-oriented. In each case, industries may be ranked by an index ranging from 1 (low-intensity) to 4 (high-intensity). Ranking of industries by technical R and D-intensity is based on the ratios of R and D expenditure to sales for various industry groups in the US in 1966. Ranking by marketing R and D-intensity is based on Census data on the ratio of advertising expenditure to value added in various industries; on the whole, marketing-oriented R and D is estimated to be most intensive in industries producing differentiated consumer goods. Table 4.2 shows how an overall measure of R and D-intensity is obtained by summing the values of the indices for technical R and D and marketing-oriented R and D. Industries for which the index exceeds 4 are classified as R and D-intensive; they are indicated by an

TABLE 4.2 Ranking of industries by R and D-intensity.

Industry	Intensity of technical innovation	Intensity of marketing innovation	Overall R and D-intensity
Oil	3	2	5*
Motor vehicles	3	3	6*
Rubber	3	2	5*
Tobacco	2	3	5*
Paper	1	2	3
Chemicals	4	2	6*
Aircraft	4	1	5*
Iron and steel	2	1	3
Food and drink	2	3	5*
Packaging	1	3	4
Textiles	1	3	4
Electrical engineering	4	2	6*
Non-electrical engineering	3	2	5*
Non-ferrous metals	1	1	2
Miscellaneous	2	2	4
Conglomerates, type I	2	3	5*
Conglomerates, type II	2	2	4

asterisk in the right-hand column of Table 4.2. Firms classified to these industries are assumed to be R and D-intensive.

The growth of a firm is estimated by the proportional change in the value of sales over the five-year period 1967–72, with 1967 as the base year. The profitability of a firm is measured by the ratio of profits to assets in 1967, and the size of the firm by the value of sales in 1967. Capital-intensity is measured by the ratio of assets to sales in 1967; this measure corresponds fairly closely to the 'average period of production', and is more appropriate than the capital–labour ratio as an index of the incentive to vertical integration. Capital includes working capital, which may be very significant in materials-processing industries.

Data on the value of sales in 1967 and 1972, profits in 1967 and assets in 1967 were collected from the *Fortune* lists. Sales figures include service and rental revenues, but exclude non-operating revenues such as dividends and interest received. Sales of subsidiaries are included whenever they are consolidated in the published accounts. Assets are measured by the value of the operating assets at the end of the year, net of depreciation. Profits are income net of taxes and net of extraordinary credits and charges.

Information on the nationality of the parent firm was also collected from *Fortune*. All except 15 firms can be classified to one of the ten countries shown in Table 4.3. The table shows that the distribution of the firms by source countries is very uneven, with countries such as Italy and Switzerland having

TABLE 4.3 Frequency distribution of firms by nationality of parent.

Nation	Number of firms
United States	264
United Kingdom	41
Japan	42
France	16
West Germany	20
Benelux	8
Italy	5
Switzerland	7
Canada	11
Sweden	5
Others	15
Total	434

only five and seven firms respectively. Of the remaining 15 firms, four are international joint ventures and the remainder are based in Austria, Argentina, Australia, India, Netherlands Antilles, Spain, South Africa and Zambia.

The multinationality of a firm is measured by the estimated proportion of the value of sales attributable to production abroad. The estimates were compiled from a variety of sources, some published, e.g. company accounts, and some unpublished, notably the replies to a questionnaire to which about 30 per cent of firms responded. Wherever possible, two or more sources were compared; subsequent checks with figures given by the UN[2] have largely confirmed the estimates.

4.3 The hypotheses

The theory developed in Chapter 2 analyses the multinationality of the firm in two logically distinct stages. The first stage considers the factors which govern the internalisation of markets. By examining the intermediate-product markets in which the firm participates, the theory predicts the optimal degree of internalisation for the firm. It is suggested that the main factors governing internalisation are industry-specific; in particular (i) the significance of knowledge flows and the difficulties of licensing knowledge, and (ii) the significance of time-lags in the production process. The first group of factors encourages the integration of production, marketing and R and D, and is likely to be of greatest significance where expenditure on R and D is a high proportion of total costs. The second factor encourages the vertical integration of production, and is likely to be most significant where production is capital-intensive.

The second stage of the analysis suggests that, *prima facie*, internalisation of markets leads to internationalisation of the firm. The theory therefore predicts that:

(1) Firms which are R and D-intensive or capital-intensive will have an above-average degree of multinationality.

The impact of internalisation of internationalisation is modified by region- and nation-specific factors. An important barrier to internationalisation is the cost of communication between plants, which increases with the geographical and 'social'

[2] Op. cit. Appendix, Table 3.

distance between the regions involved, and with international differences in language, legal and financial institutions, etc. Because detailed information on host-country investments of individual firms is not generally available (see section 4.2) a testable hypothesis must be framed in terms of the source country alone. This suggests the hypothesis that

(2) Multinationality will be greater for firms based in traditionally open economies which form part of a much wider social and ethnic grouping than for firms based in traditionally closed economies which are socially and politically isolated.

For R and D-intensive firms further consequences of internalisation can be deduced. According to section 2.4 internalisation of knowledge required for and generated by R and D leads to a relationship between the rate of growth of the firm and the scale of its R and D activities. Thus:

(3) For R and D-intensive firms, for which there is a strong incentive to internalise flows of knowledge, there will be a positive association between growth and R and D-intensity.

Further elaboration of the theory suggests a relationship between R and D-intensity and profitability. Of the factors governing the scale of R and D, some are the same for all firms, some are industry-specific, and some are firm-specific. Among the most important firm-specific factors are the parameters of demand for the firm's product – in particular the price- and quality-elasticities – the availability of basic scientific knowledge, and the height of entry barriers facing monopolistic competitors. The more favourable are these factors, the greater will be both the profitability of the firm and its optimal scale of R and D. The theory therefore predicts that:

(4) For R and D-intensive firms there will be a positive association between profitability and R and D-intensity.

Unfortunately not all of propositions (1)–(4) are directly testable because, as explained in section 4.2, information about R and D-intensity is available only at the industry level. However, there are two indirect ways of testing propositions about R and D-intensity.

The first method is appropriate when the variation in R and D-intensity of firms within an industry is small compared to the variation in average R and D-intensity between industries. In this case we can use the R and D-intensity of the industry as a surrogate for the R and D-intensity of the firm, as explained in section 4.2.

The second method is appropriate when the variation of R and D-intensity within an industry is large compared to the variation of R and D-intensity between industries. The principle is to isolate two or more variables which are believed to be related to R and D-intensity, and to test the correlation between them. Combining propositions (1), (3) and (4) yields:

(5) In R and D-intensive industries there will be positive association across firms both between multinationality and growth and between multinationality and profitability, due to the underlying influence of R and D-intensity.

It may be objected that this is not a very powerful test of the theory because other theories may well yield the same prediction. However, other theories apply equally to R and D-intensive and non-R and D-intensive firms, whereas the theory of internalisation applies particularly to R and D-intensive firms. We may therefore test the subsidiary proposition:

(6) The association between multinationality, growth and profitability is stronger in R and D-intensive industries than in non-R and D-intensive industries.

In terms of the power to discriminate between alternative theories, it is these last two hypotheses which are the most vital predictions of the theory of Chapter 2. The validity of hypotheses (5) and (6) is a crucial test of whether the theory of Chapter 2 significantly improves upon the alternative theories reviewed in Chapter 3.

4.4 Statistical methodology
It is useful to regard the hypotheses of the previous section as describing the determination of multinationality by three main groups of factors, namely country-specific, industry-specific and firm-specific factors. Hypotheses which refer to the influence of country-specific factors cannot be tested without taking account of the possible simultaneous influence of industry- and firm-specific factors; neither can industry-specific factors be tested without taking account of possible country- and firm-specific factors, and so on. For if the influence on multinationality of one set of variables were examined when all other variables were omitted from the analysis, then correlation between the

included and the omitted variables could generate seriously misleading results.

Unfortunately, while it is important to consider simultaneously all potential influences on multinationality, many of these influences are unmeasurable. However, in the case of country- and industry-specific variables it is possible to allow for their influence on multinationality by including in the analysis an appropriate set of dummy variables, which take on a value of unity for firms in the respective country or industry, and are zero otherwise. The analysis of variance reported in Table 4.4

TABLE 4.4 Explanatory power and significance of country-, industry- and firm-specific factors, as indicated by an analysis of the variance of multinationality.

Factor	Percentage of the variance explained	F-statistic	Degrees of freedom	Significance (%)
Country-specific	} 39	16.02	10	407	1
Industry-specific		5.61	16	407	1
Firm-specific	61			

suggests that country-specific factors are of paramount importance in determining multinationality, and that industry-specific factors are also important, though to a lesser degree. The following tables therefore report only those results which take full account of both country- and industry-specific factors. The analysis of variance also suggests that the influence of firm-specific factors is very considerable. However, it seems reasonable to assume that variation in firm-specific factors will tend to average out across countries and across industries, so that correlation between firm-specific variables and country- and industry-specific variables will not be a problem.

4.5   The tests

Evidence on the first hypothesis of section 4.3 is presented in Table 4.5. The regression results confirm that on average the degree of multinationality is higher in R and D-intensive industries and for capital-intensive firms. With country-specific effects eliminated, R and D-intensity increases the average degree of multinationality by more than 7 per cent and capital-intensity increases it by more than 3 per cent (see bottom line of table).

TABLE 4.5 Estimated coefficients and *t*-values of R and D-intensity and capital-intensity in the least-squares regressions of multinationality on country dummies and permutations of R and D-intensity and capital intensity.

Equation number	Independent variables	
	R and D-intensity	Capital-intensity
1	7.15	—
	(4.41)**	
2	—	2.35
		(1.25)
3	7.45	3.25
	(4.58)**	(1.76)*

Notes: The estimated coefficient is shown on the top line and the sample *t*-statistic below it. A single asterisk indicates that the coefficient differs from zero at 10 per cent significance in a two-tailed test; a double asterisk indicates 1 per cent significance.

Given the variation in the sample, both these changes are significantly different from zero.

A more interesting way of presenting the effects of R and D-intensity is shown in the first column of Table 4.6, which gives the variation across industries of the average degree of multinationality. Multinationality is measured net of country-specific effects, but gross of capital-intensity effects, whose exclusion would make negligible difference to the quoted figures. Firms in oil, chemicals and non-electrical engineering – all R and D-intensive industries – are very significantly more multinational than those in the control group (miscellaneous manufacturing), while the only industry very significantly less multinational than the control group is iron and steel, a non-R and D-intensive industry. However, there are a number of special cases which warrant further study.

The motor vehicle industry is less multinational than average, a fact which not only conflicts with our theory but which is also contrary to popular preconception. This illustrates the dangers of generalising from two particular companies – the US giants General Motors and Ford – and ignoring the behaviour of the smaller but more numerous European and Japanese manufacturers, which have very low degrees of multi-nationality. One possible explanation of the low multinationality of European manufacturers is that they tend to serve smaller, more specialised markets where the optimal size of plant is

TABLE 4.6 Estimated coefficients and *t*-values of industry dummies in the least-squares regressions of multinationality, growth, profitability and capital-intensity on industry and country dummy variables.

	Dependent variables			
Industries	*Multi-nationality*	*Growth*	*Profit-ability*	*Capital-intensity*
R and D-intensive				
Oil	17.09	27.88	0.43	0.44
	(5.06)**	(2.70)**	(0.57)	(5.29)**
Motor vehicles	−1.59	32.16	−1.87	−0.18
	(−0.37)	(2.48)*	(1.94)*	(−1.67)*
Rubber	10.82	0.79	−1.18	−0.19
	(1.65)*	(0.04)	(−0.79)	(−1.19)
Tobacco	11.97	57.19	1.72	0.43
	(1.80)*	(2.82)**	(1.14)	(2.63)**
Chemicals	12.79	15.65	1.53	0.16
	(4.06)**	(1.63)	(2.14)*	(1.99)*
Aircraft	−8.13	−50.21	−1.89	−0.36
	(−1.40)	(−2.84)**	(−1.44)	(−2.51)*
Food and drink	1.54	16.46	0.44	−0.31
	(0.48)	(1.69)*	(0.61)	(−4.03)
Electrical engineering	3.26	19.70	0.02	−0.17
	(1.09)	(2.17)*	(0.03)	(−2.26)
Non-electrical engineering	9.55	17.31	−0.26	−0.02
	(3.34)**	(1.98)*	(−0.40)	(0.33)
Conglomerates, type I	3.88	4.91	−0.22	−0.01
	(1.22)	(0.51)	(0.30)	(−0.10)
Non-R and D-intensive				
Paper	4.36	6.90	−0.04	0.10
	(0.97)	(0.50)	(−0.04)	(0.89)
Iron and steel	−12.62	−1.24	−1.15	0.37
	(−3.44)**	(−0.11)	(−1.38)	(4.14)
Packaging	8.36	3.26	−0.26	−0.02
	(1.35)	(0.17)	(0.19)	(0.13)
Textiles	−4.39	−1.65	−0.82	−0.16
	(−0.98)	(−0.12)	(−0.81)	(1.46)
Non-ferrous metals	7.87	−4.71	0.91	0.39
	(1.85)*	(0.36)	(0.95)	(3.72)
Conglomerates, type II	−1.49	23.61	−1.29	−0.01
	(−0.39)	(2.05)*	(−1.51)	(−0.13)

Note: See Table 4.5.

large relative to the overall level of demand, so that investment in branch plants is uneconomic compared with exporting. The low multinationality of the Japanese industry – even when country-specific effects have been accounted for – might be attributable to the relative infancy of the industry.

Another interesting case is the aircraft industry, which

although R and D-intensive is not at all multinational. The explanation almost certainly lies in the strategic value of the industry to national security; the need for independent control and confidentiality in defence industries induces governments to patronise indigenous firms.

Finally, it should be noted that there are two basically similar industries which exhibit very different degrees of multinationality. Both the iron and steel and non-ferrous metals industries are capital-intensive, non-R and D-intensive industries, but multinationality is 20 per cent higher in non-ferrous metals. To a certain extent this may be accounted for by the classification to non-ferrous metals of one or two R and D-intensive and highly multinational firms, such as the major aluminium producers. Another possible explanation lies in the fairly even geographical spread of iron ore and its contiguity to basic energy sources, in contrast to the typically highly concentrated deposits of non-ferrous ores, and their remoteness from complementary energy sources; as a consequence of this, a given degree of vertical integration may yield a much lower degree of multinationality in iron and steel than in non-ferrous metals.

The second hypothesis concerns the variation of the degree of multinationality with the nationality of the parent firm. Table 4.7 shows the mean difference between the percentage degree of multinationality of firms of various non-US nationalities and the multinationality of US firms. It shows that UK, Swiss and Benelux-based firms are very significantly more multinational than US firms, as are the Italian firms to a lesser degree. This result can be partially explained by the relatively small geographical areas of these countries, which means that in their case a given degree of regional diversification will produce an above-average degree of multinationality. However, the results also support the hypothesis that multinationality will be greater for firms in traditionally open economies which form part of a much wider social and ethnic grouping. The converse of this view is corroborated by the experience of the Japanese, whose firms are significantly less multinational than US firms although Japan's geographical area is very small relative to that of the US; Japan on the other hand was until recently fairly isolated and had relatively underdeveloped trading relations.

TABLE 4.7 Estimated coefficients and *t*-values of country dummies in the least-squares regression of multinationality on industry and country dummy variables.

Countries	Coefficient and t-value
United Kingdom	12.38
	(4.69)**
Japan	−14.60
	(5.59)**
France	3.25
	(0.88)
West Germany	−0.48
	(−0.12)
Benelux	39.76
	(6.92)**
Italy	13.80
	(1.95)
Switzerland	43.60
	(6.77)**
Canada	−1.02
	(−0.21)
Sweden	10.02
	(1.41)
Others	1.41
	(0.33)

Note: See Table 4.5.

It might be objected that these results may simply reflect the industrial composition of the countries, and have nothing to do with their degree of isolation. However, this objection has been met by removing all industry-specific factors in the degree of multinationality before carrying out the across-country analysis. As a matter of fact such adjustment makes relatively little difference to the measured country-specific effects, although the converse does not hold for industry-specific effects.

The remaining hypotheses concern the relationship between growth and profitability on the one hand and R and D-intensity on the other. In testing these hypotheses there are two main options, as explained in section 4.3.

The first is test whether, at the industry level, growth and profitability are higher in R and D-intensity industries than elsewhere. The results presented in Table 4.6 lend some support to the view that growth is linked to R and D-intensity. The fastest-growing firms are in oil, motor vehicles, tobacco, food and drink, electrical engineering and non-electrical engineering

– all R and D-intensive industries. The most prominent exception is the aircraft industry, which although very R and D-intensive has the slowest-growing firms in the sample. An obvious factor influencing the growth of the aircraft industry over the period 1967–72 was the reducing demand for military aircraft which was not fully absorbed by an increase in demand for civilian aircraft. However, other industries have been faced with static or declining demand, e.g. tobacco, but their firms have still succeeded in growing. The difference in the responses of firms in the two industries is probably accounted for by differences in the types of skill involved in R and D, and consequent differences in ability to diversify. Because of their very specific technical skills aircraft manufacturers were not in a position to maintain growth by diversifying into other product groups, nor were they able to rationalise by international merger, because of government-imposed barriers. On the other hand the general marketing skills of the tobacco industry, coupled with the absence of barriers to international investment, have allowed tobacco firms to maintain growth by diversifying both across industries and across countries.

Variations in profitability across industries appear to be very small and there is no obvious connection with R and D-intensity; firms in chemicals were the most profitable and firms in motor vehicles the least profitable. The results are broadly consistent with the view that, in the long run, rates of profitability in different industries are equalised by entry and exit. The higher profitability in chemicals and pharmaceuticals may be explained either as a consequence of barriers to entry, or as a premium associated with the high level of risk in the industry.

The second method of testing the relationships between growth, profitability and R and D-intensity is to test whether there are significant positive associations between growth and multinationality and between profitability and multinationality which are stronger in R and D-intensive industries than elsewhere. It is appropriate to analyse the association between each pair of variables conditional upon the value of the third, and also conditional on the size of the firm. The relevant technique is partial-correlation analysis. Table 4.8 exhibits the *t*-values associated with second-order partial correlations between multinationality and growth, multinationality and profitability and

TABLE 4.8 *t*-values associated with the second-order partial correlations between multinationality and growth, profitability and size for R and D-intensive firms and non-R and D-intensive firms.

Sample	Number of observations	Variables		
		Growth	*Profitability*	*Size*
R and D-intensive	209	1.75*	2.45*	3.50**
Non-R and D-intensive	144	0.29	1.77*	0.55

Note: A single asterisk denotes significance at 10 per cent, a double asterisk significance at 1 per cent.

multinationality and size for both R and D-intensive firms and non-R and D intensive firms. The results strongly support the hypothesis that positive partial associations exist between multinationality on the one hand and growth and profitability on the other, and that the associations are stronger for R and D-intensive firms.

It is interesting to note that among R and D-intensive firms size is strongly associated with multinationality. One possible explanation is that R and D-intensive firms are typically horizontally integrated, and the pace of centralised product development determines the multiplicity of branch plants required for adaptation of the product to local conditions; thus the size of the firm, along with the other variables, is determined by the scale of R and D, and is therefore positively associated with them.

Finally, it is interesting to test whether R and D-intensity is the only factor responsible for the observed associations between multinationality, growth, profitability and size. The theory of factor analysis suggests an approximate test for the number of unmeasurable factors responsible for an observed pattern of correlation, namely that the number of factors is equal to the number of latent roots of the correlation matrix which exceed unity. Table 4.9(*a*) shows the matrix of correlations between the four variables once country-specific and industry-specific effects (including the effect of the average R and D-intensity of the industry) have been eliminated from each of the variables. We note in passing that the form of the matrix is fairly typical: large firms tend to grow more slowly than small firms (an effect partially due to the way the sample is selected) while profitability is largely independent of size.

Table 4.9(*b*) shows the latent roots of the correlation matrix and their corresponding principal components. It suggests that there are two unmeasurable factors, the first of which varies in a manner similar to an average of multinationality, profitability and size and the second of which varies positively with growth and profitability and negatively with size. The first factor probably represents the impact of intra-industry variation in R and D-intensity as explained above.

TABLE 4.9 Factor analysis of the residuals of multinationality, growth, profitability and size from regressions of these variables on country and industry dummy variables. (*a*) Correlation matrix. (*b*) Latent roots and the corresponding principal components.

(*a*)

	Multinationality	Growth	Profitability	Size
Multinationality	1.0	0.098	0.118	0.228
Growth	0.098	1.0	0.118	−0.117
Profitability	0.118	0.118	1.0	0.064
Size	0.228	−0.117	0.064	1.0

(*b*)

Number	Latent root	Coefficient on			
		Multinationality	Growth	Profitability	Size
1	1.29	0.67	0.20	0.47	0.54
2	1.14	−0.04	0.76	0.36	−0.54
3	0.87	0.44	0.41	−0.80	−0.00
4	0.69	−0.60	0.47	−0.09	0.64

The second factor may represent influences on growth and profitability to which smaller firms are particularly sensitive, such as windfall gains from unexpected changes in market conditions. However, this is highly conjectural, and merely emphasises the need for further work in this area.

4.6 Problems of mis-specification

The results reported in the preceding section appear to confirm the major hypotheses derived from Chapter 2. However, before accepting that the sample data are consistent with the main predictions of the theory, it is important to consider the sensitivity of our inferences to mis-specification of the underlying statistical relationships. The methods of inference we have used are standard techniques of multivariate statistical theory. Under certain well-known assumptions the estimates and tests used are respectively maximum likelihood and likelihood ratio, and therefore possess a number of desirable properties.[3]

In the present context the most questionable of these assumptions are that (i) all underlying relationships are linear, (ii) the net impact of omitted variables on multinationality is normally distributed, and (iii) all variables are measured without error.

The importance of non-linearity has been argued by Rowthorn,[4] whose results suggest amongst other things that the size of the firm has a non-linear impact on its rate of growth. However, detailed work on our sample, reported elsewhere,[5] has failed to confirm this view; the non-linearities reported by Rowthorn appear to be due to the omission of multinationality as an influence on the growth of the firm.

It is easily established by chi-square and Neyman–Barton tests on the regression residuals that the estimated impact on multinationality of the omitted variables does not follow a normal distribution, a result which is closely allied to the fact the degree of multinationality is restricted to the range between 0 and 100 per cent. Although t-tests are relatively robust to deviations from normality, wherever practicable the reported significance levels were checked using non-parametric tests based on rank correlations. Although the results of the tests sometimes differ in detail, the overall nature of the inferences is unaffected.

The potential impact of measurement errors is more serious. It is well known that errors in the measurement of firms' operating assets are large in many cases, and that sales figures are often a poor indicator of the scale of the firm's production. Additional complications arise because the key variables in our analysis are measured in ratio form, with the numerator of one variable sometimes appearing as the numerator or denominator of another variable, and vice versa; the role of assets in the measurement of profitability and of capital-intensity, and the role of sales in the measurement of size and growth are cases in point. Errors in the measurement of ratio variables can produce serious biases. However, if an upper bound on the variance

[3] The basic reference on classical multivariate analysis is M. G. Kendall and A. Stuart, *The Advanced Theory of Statistics*, 4th ed., vol. 2 (London, 1961).

[4] Op. cit., ch. 2.

[5] J. H. Dunning, P. J. Buckley and R. D. Pearce, *The World's Largest Firms*, mimeo (Reading, 1975).

of the measurement error is known, then bounds can be calculated for the asymptotic biases in the estimated parameters and their associated test statistics. Trial calculations reveal that the biases produced by measurement errors would have little or no tendency to produce misleading confirmatory evidence for our hypotheses.

Finally, it could be argued that using more sophisticated techniques our estimates and tests could be improved upon further. In certain cases our estimates and tests use only a limited amount of the information contained in the sample. Full information estimates and tests could be obtained by simultaneously estimating the impact of country- and industry-specific factors on multinationality, growth, profitability and size and iterating the procedure, using the correlations between the residuals of these variables to improve successive estimates until convergence is obtained. However, the results which emerge from such a procedure are only marginally different from those reported in the text, and in view of the greater simplicity of interpretation and verification, we decided to base our inferences on the limited information results reported earlier.

4.7 Conclusion
A statistical study of the world's largest firms over the period 1967–72 confirms the major hypotheses derived from Chapter 2, in particular the relationship between multinationality, growth and profitability which stems from the internalisation of flows of knowledge in R and D-intensive firms. The nationality of the parent firm is a very significant influence on the behaviour of an MNE, and it appears particularly strongly in the influence of the degree of isolation of the source economy on the firm's degree of multinationality. Other factors which have a discernible, but not very large influence on multinationality include the capital-intensity of the production process and the evenness of the geographical spread of key resources in the industry.

The short-comings of the available data severely restrict the power of the statistical tests, but there is no reason to believe that the confirmatory nature of the tests is in any way attributable to errors of specification.

5 Predictions and Policy Implications

5.1 Introduction

A rational long-term policy toward the MNE, and toward international trade and investment in general, must be based upon an analysis of the underlying forces in the world economy. A theory of these forces and of how they have influenced the growth of the MNE was presented in the earlier chapters of this book. The present chapter shows how the theory can be used to predict the future evolution of MNEs and appraise the probable effects of various policies toward them.

5.2 The pattern of future growth

We have argued that the main dynamic in the post-war growth of the MNE has been a structural shift in favour of technology-based goods, which has significantly increased investment in R and D. The structural shift has been induced both from the demand side and the supply side. On the demand side the main factors have been rising consumer incomes and increased sophistication of tastes, and high levels of government spending on defence and on prestige projects; on the supply side the main factor has been the increased availability of skilled labour.

It seems unlikely that, in the foreseeable future, investment in technical R and D will attain, in real terms, the levels of the fifties and sixties. The main reason is a reduction in the demand for new technology-based goods. To begin with, a lasting consequence of the energy crisis is likely to be a reduction of the rate of growth of incomes in the developed economies, so that fewer new wants for sophisticated consumer goods will be created. Furthermore the recent downward trend in expenditure on arms and space race projects is likely to continue in the

102

developed countries, partly as a result of more slowly rising incomes but also as a consequence of deliberate restraint on the growth of public expenditure in mixed economies. On the supply side a relative glut of trained labour is already emerging in several countries, and the scope for further improvement in the conditions of labour supply to R and D are thus fairly limited.

Nevertheless three possible areas of continued growth through technical R and D can be distinguished. The first concerns selected industries which are currently favoured by changing world prices, e.g. producers of energy-saving products, developers of technology for marginal oil fields, etc. The second concerns industries which are able to capitalise on continuing breakthroughs in basic research, e.g. bioengineering. The third concerns industries producing income-elastic goods for which demand can be expected to expand as incomes in developing countries increase.

In the first two cases the potential sources of growth are very similar to those which existed on a much wider scale in the fifties and sixties, and a broadly similar pattern of evolution can be expected. Most of the firms in these industries are at present fairly small, and are pursuing rival – though to some extent complementary – avenues of research. Competition between them will tend to select out a few 'world-beating' technologies, on the basis of which their proprietors will expand to the status of large-scale international producers.

In the third case – that of an increasing demand for an existing income-elastic good – it must be recognised that the implications of a widening scope for an existing technology are different from those of a continuing demand for new technology. A widening scope for an existing technology places the emphasis on the adaptation of a general technology to a local environment, which requires different skills from the development of a wholly new technology. The relevant skill-mix includes knowledge of how to do business in the local environment, ability to debug and redesign equipment, and an ability to liaise simultaneously with a large number of interested parties. It is by no means obvious that firms with specific technical skills in the development of new products also possess these more general managerial skills. It has been demonstrated in the past that certain firms do have the ability to adapt to changing conditions by acquiring a new set of skills. But many firms do not have this ability. For those that do not, the outlook is fairly bleak. When the firm's flow of new technical knowledge reduces to a level where the benefits of internalisation are less than the overhead costs of the firm's communication system then the economic rationale for the internalisation of knowledge is eliminated, and the basis for multinationality is undermined. It becomes economic for the MNE to sell off foreign plants to indigenous producers and to license technology to them as required, rather than to maintain a world-wide organisation for the diffusion of technology.

Thus for firms with specific technical skills which cannot be adapted to changing circumstances, the theory predicts a reduction in the pace of research activity and an increasing resort to licensing as a means of exploiting the results of research; for such firms we may therefore anticipate lower rates of growth and profitability, and a reduction in the multinationality of their operations.

When we turn from technical skills to marketing skills there seems to be little reason to modify the conclusions of the preceding analysis. It is important to distinguish between marketing skills adapted to *developed*-country environments and those adapted to *developing*-country environments. The reduced rate of growth of incomes in developed countries will mean less demand for skills in the pioneering work of innovating new products in advanced markets, but the acceleration of income levels in developing countries relative to developed countries will mean increased demand for skills in consolidating the position of existing products by adapting them to less advanced markets. Firms with marketing expertise in developing economies are therefore likely to find an increasingly wide range of products suitable for adaptation to their markets. The rights to these products will typically be acquired by licensing from firms who are proprietors of goods already innovated in advanced markets, but whose marketing expertise does not extend to developing countries, or whose management lacks the flexibility to acquire such expertise. Thus the marketing-based MNE of the future will typically be a firm with general skills in the adaptation of existing products to the market environments of developing countries; firms without such skills, or who are unable to acquire them, will confine their foreign investments to developed countries, and service developing economies by licensing.

5.3 Attitudes of host governments

We have argued in the previous section that in future many MNEs will be characterised by general skills in the adaptation of products and technologies to developing countries. An increasingly important ingredient of these skills will be the ability to liaise effectively with host governments in the planning and day to day operation of production activities.

There is a definite trend toward concerted action among developing countries in restricting the discretion of foreign firms. Sometimes host-government intervention takes the form of statutory restrictions on, say, the proportion of foreign nationals in senior administrative grades; in other cases permission to invest is dependent on a measure of government participation in the project, or on some form of joint-venture arrangement with an indigenous producer.

The attitudes underlying these restrictions have been formed as a response to a number of difficulties, both real and imagined, some of which are outlined below. An understanding of these attitudes, and an ability to resolve the problems from which they arise will be an important attribute of the successful foreign investor in the future.

A major problem for the host government is that the foreign subsidiary's ultimate locus of authority is in another country. This means that when international political conflicts emerge, concerning for example the supply of strategic goods to third countries, the source-country government may attempt to use the MNE's internal channels of authority to influence decisions in the host country. Alternatively, strategic information collected by the foreign subsidiary may be channelled through to corporate headquarters and from there to the source-country government. It would appear that a prerequisite for maintaining good relations between the host government and the MNE is that the autonomy of the subsidiary should be guaranteed by the appropriate degree of decentralisation within the firm.

Even where the autonomy of the subsidiary is sufficient to safeguard the strategic interests of the host-country government, conflicts may still arise over issues of national importance. The foreign subsidiary may be involved in activities with considerable social and environmental externalities, e.g. training labour, inducing regional migration of workers, depleting unpriced natural resources, etc. The success of the host government in harmonising these activities with its own social and economic policies may depend crucially on the commitment of the subsidiary management to host-country interests. In many cases nowadays, managers – whether foreign or local – appear to behave as though their principal alliegance is to the firm. This is particularly true of managers who are 'locked in' to the firm through pension schemes, etc. and whose international mobility within the firm is much greater than their inter-firm mobility within the host country. In order to co-operate effectively with host governments these managers will need to become sympathetic to the host-country point of view, and to be adept at assessing to what extent, and in what way, acquiescence in government policy is consistent with, or even enhances, long-run profit-maximisation for the firm.

Finally, it appears that in the popular view the major threat of foreign investment is the diffusion of an alien ideology or way of life. Objections often concern the nature of the product and the method by which it is marketed. Wider criticisms are sometimes made of mass-production methods, but there is little evidence that on the shop-floor foreign firms are considered bad employers; on the contrary wages and conditions of work in foreign-owned plants often compare favourably with those of their indigenous competitors. To the extent that governments are influenced by such views, MNEs may find it increasingly important to justify their products and production methods in the light of social criteria endorsed by the host government. An ability to harmonise corporate strategy with these views will be a key ingredient in successful multinational operations.

We conclude that negotiations with host governments over the external effects of foreign direct investments will absorb an increasing proportion of managerial resources, and that skill in liaising with host governments will become an important attribute of successful MNEs. Foreign direct investment will increasingly involve government participation or joint-venture arrangements with indigenous producers. Firms with technical and marketing skills who are unable to co-operate effectively with host governments or who find it difficult to administer joint-venture arrangements may prefer to license their know-how to firms with the requisite complementary skills. Thus the attitudes of host countries toward foreign direct investment may reinforce the movement toward licensing among firms with very specific skills in technology or product development.

5.4 Attitudes of governments in source countries
We have argued above that the prospects for MNEs with highly specialised skills in the development of new products and new technologies are not very favourable. A reduced growth of demand will result in lower growth and profitability and thereby induce a contraction of the scale of R and D activities. The reduced scale of R and D, combined with an increasing need for skills in liaising with host governments, may in turn tip the balance on economic grounds away from foreign direct investment and toward licensing.

Both of these trends will be most unwelcome to the managers of the firms concerned, since they reduce the potential scope for managerial activity and threaten earnings prospects. It might be argued that these trends will therefore be resisted, and that despite the economic incentives acting on profitability, managements will prefer to maintain a large scale of R and D and to continue to operate abroad. However, this view ignores the constraints on managerial discretion which stem from the competitive pricing of the firm's equity in the stock market. Firms which deviate too far from profit-maximisation will become susceptible to takeover, since a 'company doctor' or 'promoter' could earn a substantial reward simply by acquiring control, reorganising the management on profit-maximising lines, and selling off all or part of the reorganised firm. The reward would be equal to the increase in the company valuation due to the increase in the expected stream of profits, less the cost of the takeover.

However when considering the competitive constraints on management the attitude of the source government is very important. Rationalisation of R and D activities on an inter-national scale may well involve the merger of firms of different nationalities, or the outright takeover of a domestically owned

MNE by a foreign firm. If the R and D activities are regarded as of strategic importance, either from an economic or political point of view, then the source government may consider it to be in its interests to prevent the merger or takeover. Sometimes a merger with another domestically owned firm may also be outlawed on the grounds that it conflicts with competition policy in domestic markets. In such cases the management of the MNE may be effectively insulated from competitive pressures through the intervention of the source government, and so may remain free to pursue suboptimal policies of excessive R and D expenditure and overinvestment abroad. It is ironic that in such cases the pursuit of policies designed to promote competition through ensuring the existence of a large number of independent producers may in fact impair the competitive mechanism in the capital market and thereby enable managers to perpetuate deviations from cost-minimising conditions of supply. In fact it can be argued that policies designed to promote atomistic supply are quite inappropriate as a means of ensuring an efficient allocation of resources to R and D-based activities. If this is the case then source governments may have to rethink their competition policies if they are to deal adequately with the problems posed by the rationalisation of MNEs.

Another problem of considerable concern to host governments is the potential scope for MNEs to avoid profit taxation and evade capital controls through transfer pricing. This advantage is conferred exclusively on the MNE by its access to internal markets in which prices are essentially notional. The effect is to distort the allocation of resources in favour of the MNE. From the economic point of view the obvious solution is for the tax authorities to prescribe the use of 'arm's length' prices based on independent estimates of the underlying scarcities of the intermediate products concerned. The implementation of such a policy is fraught with practical difficulties. In principle the impact of the policy would depend on the extent to which MNEs subsidise otherwise unprofitable activities out of the profits of transfer pricing. Only if such a practice were widespread would competitive pressures seriously affect the viability of MNEs.

Another issue of importance to host governments is the extent to which MNEs are responsible for 'exporting jobs' from the source country. The crucial question is whether the location strategy of an MNE differs significantly from the strategy which would be followed by an equivalent group of independent firms. The theory of Chapter 2 suggests that the location strategy of a profit-maximising MNE is exactly the same as that for an equivalent group of independent firms, except in the following cases. The first is that of transfer pricing, where there may be an incentive for the firm to channel internal trade in certain goods through a low-tax country, thereby widening the scope of its foreign operations. The remaining cases all concern situations where the existence of an MNE will restrict the scope of foreign operations: high communications costs attributable to social and linguistic barriers, political costs due to host-country attitudes to foreign investment, and administrative costs due to unfamiliarity with internal market operations. On balance it would appear that less production is located outside the source country when the activities are MNE-owned and controlled than when production is in the hands of independent national producers. In the context of a competitive world economy, attempts to bias the MNE's production in favour of the source country will reduce the MNE's profitability *vis-a-vis* foreign indigenous producers; the theory suggests that in the long run this will lead to less investment and fewer jobs in the source country, not more.

We conclude that attempts by source-country governments to regulate transfer pricing should in principle increase efficiency by exerting competitive pressures on firms at present subsidising unprofitable production activities by this method. However, attempts to control directly the location strategies of MNE to favour investment and employment in the source country will almost certainly be counterproductive, as they will reduce the competitiveness of the MNE in foreign markets and build up foreign indigenous competitors.

5.5   The efficiency of the MNE

Our analysis has emphasised the role of the MNE as a developer and transferor of various kinds of knowledge and skill. We have argued that the main rationale for the MNE is the existence of widespread market imperfections which make the production and diffusion of knowledge and skills difficult to achieve except through internalisation. In this section we attempt to evaluate the efficiency of the MNE as a mechanism for the production and diffusion of knowledge.

Our approach is to compare the operations of MNEs in imperfect world markets with the behaviour of a hypothetical perfect-market economy. In making this comparison it is important to recognise that as a commodity knowledge exhibits two distinctive features: it is 'indivisible' and it is a 'public good'.

Because items of knowledge are indivisible all replication of knowledge-producing activities is inefficient. Unlike most products, but in common with works of art, etc., each item of knowledge is unique and indivisible. However many potential suppliers of an item of knowledge there happen to be, one of them will necessarily be first to supply the knowledge, and once this has been done the efforts of the others – both retrospectively and in the future – are rendered superfluous. Thus while the potential producers of knowledge may be many, and may compete against one another for the right to undertake production, efficiency demands that there is only one actual producer of knowledge.

Knowledge also has the property of a public good, namely that it can be supplied by one person to another without any reduction in the supplier's access to the services of the good. Acquisition of knowledge represents a once-for-all change in the state of mind, and once this had been effected the knowledge can be communicated to others at no cost except the marginal resource cost of the transmission. It follows that, once produced, knowledge is no longer a scarce commodity in the economic sense. Social efficiency therefore requires that it should be diffused to all individuals or organisations who are willing to pay the marginal cost of transmission.

A market economy can reconcile the requirements of efficient production of knowledge and efficient exploitation of knowledge by the following method. Firstly, any firm is allowed to secure sole rights to acquire and exploit a particular type of knowledge by applying for the relevant rights to be auctioned off competitively by the government (or similar body). This system of competitive auction in fact guarantees that knowledge will be produced at minimum cost (in particular without duplication) and that the supply price of knowledge is equal to its cost of production. Secondly, the knowledge is exploited through discriminatory pricing, i.e. the owner of the newly produced knowledge sells to each individual or organisation a non-transferable right to utilise the knowledge, each individual or organisation being asked to pay the maximum amount they are willing to pay, but not less than the marginal social cost of transmitting the knowledge to them. When transmission costs are negligible this means that knowledge is made available to all individuals or organisations who are willing to pay any amount, however small, for use of the knowledge. In this way knowledge is made available to all individuals or organisations who value it at not less than its marginal social cost. Because of the system of competitive tendering for the rights to research, any surplus of revenue over the opportunity cost of production accrues to the government, and research is undertaken only if it yields the government a positive or zero surplus.

It is fairly clear that there are a number of practical difficulties associated with achieving an optimal production and distribution of knowledge through market forces. The difficulties are associated both with defining and enforcing the requisite proprietary rights to knowledge and with implementing discriminatory pricing. In the light of this, any practical system for organising the production and distribution of knowledge in a market economy is likely to be a 'second-best' system, since the first-best system is administratively infeasible.

When the system of the production and distribution of knowledge which relies on the MNE as a key agent is compared with the ideal system outlined above, it is possible to distinguish two major weaknesses in the MNE-based system which it may be practicable to remedy, at least partially.

The first is the replication of research activities by the leading firms in certain industries, which usually represents a wasteful use of the limited research resources in the industry. The inefficiencies tend to increase when there is a specific reward associated with being the first to discover some new knowledge, e.g. the discoverer has the right to patent protection, or is able to acquire a 'market lead'. In this case the research process tends to be speeded up unduly, as competitors race against one another to be the first to complete the research. As a result each firm tends to operate with a single large research team working on a succession of short-term projects instead of with a number of smaller research teams each working on a longer-term project. It is possible to visualise an extension of the patent system which would give firms protection not only on the results of their research but also continuing protection of their research in progress, thereby encouraging firms to rationalise their research activities among themselves and to undertake between them a variety of long-term research projects rather than simply a succession of broadly similar short-term projects.

The second major weakness of MNE-based production and distribution of knowledge is that as a consequence of the difficulties of discriminatory pricing, proprietary knowledge is offered to many individuals and organisations at a price which is well above what they are willing to pay, even though they are willing to pay more than the marginal social cost of the knowledge. In this case the diffusion of knowledge is restricted in a socially undesirable way. A possible remedy is to promote discriminatory pricing of knowledge, by permitting markets for new products and new processes to be divided up nationally and regionally. In this case the proprietor can sell a licence to service a small or marginal market at a very low price on the security that the licensee cannot attempt to supply another more profitable market as well.

Without this security the proprietor of knowledge would be unwilling to license it to another producer at a low price, however small that producer's market, because of the potential threat to other markets which may be involved. This is particularly relevant to the problems of developing countries who are anxious to acquire greater control over the exploitation of new products and processes in their countries. While an increasing measure of control over purely local production and marketing may be acceptable to foreign investors, e.g. through joint ventures, demands for unconditional licensing or for discretion over the export policy of foreign investors are likely to meet with considerable resistance, as they pose a potential threat to the world-wide viability of the investing firm. Only an improvement in the international regulation and enforcement of licensing arrangements, or a change in patent laws, will be sufficient to eliminate the role of foreign investment as a preferred means of exploiting proprietary knowledge world-wide.

5.6 Conclusion

In the future the major role of the MNE will continue to be the production and diffusion of knowledge. However, the type of knowledge which is most significant to the operations of the MNE is undergoing change. In the future there will be less reliance on very specific skills in producing new products and processes and more reliance on general skills in adapting existing products and processes to new environments. Specialised firms will tend to rely more on licensing and less on foreign investments as a means of exploiting their knowledge. The firms they license to will be international firms skilled in co-operating with foreign governments and foreign business communities, particularly those in developing countries. Joint ventures will become more prevalent as a means of harmonising the profit-maximising objectives of foreign investors with the social policies of host governments.

The future of firms specialised in industries with little demand for new products or little opportunity for developing new processes will depend on the attitudes of source-country governments. If governments intervene to prevent the international rationalisation of R and D then, far from stimulating competition, they will protect inefficient managements and encourage the perpetuation of excessive levels of R and D expenditure and foreign investment.

There is little doubt that in a world of imperfect markets the activities of MNEs in developing and transferring knowledge internationally have been beneficial to both source and host countries. Foreign investment has allowed MNEs to bypass imperfect external markets for knowledge, and thereby diminished barriers to the production and diffusion of proprietary knowledge. However, it is possible to visualise policies which would improve the external markets for knowledge, firstly by reducing the incentive to competitive duplication of R and D, and secondly by permitting more effective marketing of knowledge. The implementation of these policies would involve radical changes in the patent system and a new approach to competition policy in general. Their effect would be to encourage a rationalisation of R and D activities between competing firms and the substitution of licensing for foreign direct investment.

Index